IN THE BEGINNING GOD...

Valarie Owen

WORD OF FAITH
LEADERSHIP AND BIBLE INSTITUTE

All Scripture quotations
from the *King James Version*
of the Bible unless otherwise stated

"ALL SCRIPTURE IS GIVEN BY INSPIRATION OF GOD, AND IS PROFIT- ABLE FOR DOCTRINE, FOR REPROOF, FOR CORRECTION, FOR INSTRUCTION IN RIGHTEOUSNESS: THAT THE MAN OF GOD MAY BE PERFECT, THROUGHLY FURNISHED UNTO ALL GOOD WORKS" (II TIMOTHY 3:16).

Quotes from the Amplified Bible used by permission of the Zondervan Publishing House of Grand Rapids, Michigan.

ISBN 0-914307-00-2

Cover photo by John W. Tozier-WORD OF FAITH

CONTENTS

INTRODUCTION

The first five books in the Old Testament are called the *"Pentateuch"* which is a Greek word meaning *"five volumes."* The Jews call these books *"the Law."* In Hebrew the word *"bereshith"* means *"beginnings"* and in Greek the word for *"beginnings"* is *"genesis."* Thus, in this book called *"Genesis"* we have a book of *"beginnings."* There are many books in the Bible, but the book of Genesis is the foundation of all of them. It is often referred to as the *"seed plot"* of the entire Bible. If the book of *"beginnings"* had been lost to us, we would have no valid foundation upon which to build, for it is the progressive self-revelation of God which culminates in Christ Jesus our Lord.

We are immediately introduced to God as *"Elohim"* when we read, *"In the beginning God.. ."* which leaves no room for argument as to His eternal existence. C.H. MacKintosh worte, *"The Holy Ghost opens this sublime book in a peculiarly striking manner. He introduces us at once to God, in the essential fullness of His Being, and the solitariness of His acting. All prefatory matter is omitted. It is to God we are brought. We hear Him, as it were, breaking earth's silence, and shining in upon earth's darkness, for the purpose of developing a sphere in which He might display His eternal power and Godhead."*

There is yet another way that a Jewish man explained the first three words in Genesis to me: *"Bar-Asheet means Genesis to us: the first book of the Bible.* (Literal meaning: In the beginning), but

Hebrew words have hidden root meanings. *"Bar"* also means son. Bar-Mitzvah, which means *"son of the law."* Asheet also can mean *'set forth'*, or *'bring about.'* Here God is saying in the Hebrew language, BAR-ASHEET, I WILL SET FORTH A SON."

The Pentateuch was written by Moses under the leadership of the precious Holy Spirit. In Exodus 24:4 we read, *"and Moses wrote all the words of the Lord, and rose up early in the morning, and built an altar under the hill, and twelve pillars, according to the twelve tribes of Israel."* In Deuteronomy 31:9, we have further proof from the Word that Moses wrote the first five books of the Bible, *"And Moses wrote the law, and delivered it unto the priests, the sons of Levi, who bore the ark of the covenant of the Lord, and unto all the elders of Israel."* In Joshua 1:7-8 we read, *"Only be thou strong and very courageous, that thou mayest observe to do according to all the law, which Moses, my servant, commanded thee; turn not from it to the right hand or to the left, that thou mayest prosper withersoever thou goest. This book of the law shall not depart out of thy mouth, but thou shalt meditate therein day and night, that thou mayest observe to do according to all that is written therein; for then thou shalt make thy way prosperous, and then thou shalt have good success."*

In this book we will consider only three of the primary names of God. The most common name for Deity is God, a translation of the original *"Elohim."* The *"El"* suggests strength. The God of *"strength"* in plural form. *"Adonai"* is a Hebrew word meaning Lord. There is yet another name which was never pronounced by the Jews because of the sacredness attached to it. It has only four letters, YHWH, and the translation is *"Yahweh."* Scholars tell us that the name Jehovah (formed from those four letters) was not known to us until 1520.

There are many reasons why one should study the Old Testament, but the most important one is that Jesus Himself directed the religious leaders of His day to search the scriptures for they testified of Him. In John 5:39 we read, *"Search the scriptures: for in them ye think ye have eternal life: and they are they which testify of me."* Jesus was God's reason for the Eternal Word. In the Old Testament we study outstanding types, figures, and shadows of the Lord Jesus Christ. Everything in the Old Testament is a type of which something in the New Testament is the antetype. The unveiling of our Lord Jesus Christ begins with the first verse of Genesis, and ends with the last chapter and verse of the book of Revelation. The Bible is the unveiling of the Lamb of God slain from the foundation of the world. Only by this revelation will we fully understand Satan's vicious attacks upon the righteous *"Seed."* Jesus said to His accusers in John 5:45-47, *"Do not think that I will accuse you to the Father: there is one that accuseth you, even Moses, in whom ye trust. For had ye believed Moses, ye would have believed me: for he wrote of me. But if ye believe not his writings, how shall ye believe my words?"*

In the Old Testament redemption is promised. In the New Testament Jesus is the fulfillment of that promise. In the Old Testament many animal sacrifices were offered, but only Jesus could be that final sacrifice and atonement. Jesus is the fulfillment of every promise given in the Old Testament. Though born of the seed of David, He was the perfect and Eternal King of whom David was but a type.

At one time all the blessings of the Old Testament were limited to a nation, tribe, and familly or certain individuals; but today all that is written in the Word of God finds its fulfillment in Jesus, and we are complete in Him.

In Hebrews 1:1-3, we read, *"God, who at sundry times and in divers manners spake in time past unto the fathers by the prophets, hath in these last days spoken unto us by His Son, whom he hath appointed heir of all things, by whom also he made the worlds: Who being the brightness of his glory, and the express image of his person, and upholding all things by the word of his power, when he had by himself purged our sins, sat down on the right hand of the Majesty on high."*

Also we must study the Old Testament because it will provide for us a wealth of spiritual and material blessings. In the Amplified Bible, Psalm 1:1-3, these blessings are clearly outlined for us: *"Blessed-happy, fortunate, prosperous and enviable-is the man who walks and lives not in the counsel of the ungodly (following their advice, their plans and purposes), nor stands (submissive and inactive) in the path where sinners walk, nor sits down (to relax and rest) where the scornful (and the mockers) gather. But his delight and desire are in the law of the Lord, and on His law-the precepts, the instructions, the teachings of God — he habitually meditates (ponders and studies) by day and by night. And he shall be like a tree planted and tended) by the streams of water, ready to bring forth his fruit in its' season; his leaf also shall not fade or wither, and everything he does shall prosper (and come to maturity)."*

Since Jesus is the fulfillment of all things, we must study both the Old and the New Testament in order to gain comprehensive insight into the ways and purposes of God.

I have had the blessed privilege of teaching the Old Testament at Word of Faith Leadership Institute to serious students of the Word for the past six years; to them I lovingly dedicate this work.

This book is not set forth as a critical verse-by-verse analysis of Genesis, but as an enjoyable story for the layman who has vowed over and over to read the entire Bible in one year, only to discover Genesis to be a stumbling block to all those good intentions; soon the entire project was abandoned due to the lack of time to do even the most basic amount of research. It is my prayer that all who read this simple outline will take heart and begin with verse 1, *"In the beginning . . ."* I want this story of the development of the Hebrew people to be as thrilling and exciting to others, as it has become to me in the past few years, and a real faith-builder in our heritage which for so long has been neglected.

PART I
CREATION
1. IN THE BEGINNING
(Genesis 1)   (3975 B.C.)

Genesis is the book of "Beginnings." God is the absolute originator and initiator in all things. All things begin with Him and work down towards man. He offers no argument as to who He is. Paul tells us that without faith it is impossible to please God. In Hebrews 11:6, we read, *"But without faith it is impossible to please Him: for he that cometh to God must believe that He is, and that He is a rewarder of them that diligently seek Him."* In Psalm 90:2 we have further scriptural proof that our God is from everlasting to everlasting: *"Before the mountains were brought forth, or even thou hadst formed the earth and the world, even from the everlasting to everlasting, thou art God."* In Isaiah 45:18 we have those words repeated: *"For thus saith the Lord that created the heavens God himself that formed the earth and the world, even from everlasting to everlasting, thou art God."* As for God's part, that settles it.

If we do not recognize our Lord to be the creator of all things, we tend to limit Him as to His ability to take absolute control of our lives; and we lack understanding as to why this world was created in the first place.

Verse 1: In the beginning God created the heaven and the earth.

Verse 2: And the earth was without form, and void; and darkness was upon the face of the deep. And the Spirit of God moved upon the face of the waters.

1

To "create" is to call into existence something out of nothing. The Hebrew word *"bara,"* used exclusively of God, denotes a "creative" act without the use of pre-existing materials. In other words, a carpenter can make a table out of wood, but he cannot make the wood. We need to show a distinction between the two words, or we will fail to understand the full meaning of "creation" as set forth in Genesis. Was it not our God who called those things that be not into existence according to Romans 4:17, *"(As it is written, I have made thee a father of many nations,) before him whom he believed, even God, who quickeneth the dead, and calleth those things which be not as though they were."* In Hebrews 11:3, we read, *"Through faith we understand that the worlds were framed by the word of God, so that things which are seen were not made of things which do appear."*

God has invested in us the same power to speak things into existence; but we speak forth from that which He Himself has already "created", as man can never act independently of his Creator. In 2 Corinthians 4:13, we read, *"We have the same spirit of faith, according as it is written, I believed, and therefore have I spoken; we also believed and therefore speak."*

None but an Omnipotent God could create the *"heaven and the earth."* One writer said that during the past eternity God was alone, self sufficient, and in need of nothing. Again, we are confronted with the truth that God has always lived in the vastness of His eternity; and it was from there that the Trinity (Elohim) planned the Redemptive Program.

THE PRE-EXISTENT CHRIST

Let us consider the pre-existent Christ in line with the story of "creation" and "redemption." The Son of God, the Eternal Word and Wisdom of the Father, was with God when He created. He moved and breathed, and spoke as the Father Himself moved and breathed and spoke by His Eternal Spirit, and the worlds as we see them now came into existence. In Ephesians 3:9, we read, *"And to make all men see what is the fellowship of the mystery, which from the beginning of the world hath been hid in God who created all things by Jesus Christ."* And in Colossians 1:16-17, we are assured that by Him all things were created: *"For by him were all things created, that are in heaven, and that are in the earth, visible and invisible, whether they be thrones, or dominions, or principalities, or powers: all things were created by him, and for him: And he is before all things, and by him all things consist."*

In the Amplified Bible we read in Romans 11:36 that all things were by Him and originate from Him: *"For from Him and through Him and to Him are all things. For all things originate with Him and come from Him; all things live through Him, and all things center in and tend to consummate and to end in Him. To Him be glory forever! Amen-so be it."*

John the beloved Apostle recorded that Jesus was One with the Father even in the Eternity past. He was the Word, and the Word became flesh and dwelt among us. In John 1:1, 3, 10, we read, *"In the beginning was the Word, and the Word was with God, and the Word was God. The same was in the*

3

beginning with God. All things were made by him; and without him was not anything made that was made. He was in the world, and the world was made by him, and the world knew him not."

Thus, Jesus was with the Father before the worlds were spoken into existence; for He was, *"the Lamb slain from the foundation of the world..." (Revelation 13:8); "And I beheld ... a Lamb that was slain ..." (Revelation 5:12); "Worthy is the Lamb that was slain..." (Revelation 7:14); "... washed their robes, and made them white in the blood of the Lamb ..." (Revelation 12:11).*

Over that waste — that nothingness, Elohim moved to create, and the Eternal Spirit of God brooded over the face of the waters. The "brooding" of the Holy Spirit over the face of the waters typifies in its foreshadowment the Incarnation of Jesus: *"And the angel answered and said unto her, The Holy Ghost shall come upon thee and the power of the Highest shall overshadow thee; therefore that holy thing which shall be born of thee shall be called the Son of God" (Luke 1:35).* Also, the word "brooding" typifies the work of the Holy Spirit in the hearts of men as He convicts of sin. Jesus wept over the sins of the city of Jerusalem, comparing His feelings to that of a mother hen brooding over her nest: *"O Jerusalem, Jerusalem, which killest the prophets, and stonest them that are sent unto thee; how often would I have gathered thy children together, as a hen doth gather her brood under her wings, and ye would not" (Luke 13:34)!*

Elohim spoke faith-filled words full of power and energy, and His Word created a universe of flowering beauty and variety. What less than Almighty Strength could bring all things that now exist out of nothing, including darkened souls?

DAY ONE: LIGHT

Verse 3: And God said, Let there be light: and there was light.

When God spoke, the light appeared. He saw that the light was good, and He divided the light from the darkness. He gave the light the name DAY, and the darkness He called NIGHT. We find that the darkness pre-existed.

Now we have entered into a study of the BEGINNING of time upon the earth. This was God's first day of work in connection with developing a world in which to place a family. Together, the light and the darkness formed the first day. This light would seem to be like our word "illuminate," or light, as opposed to darkness. He said it was good.

DAY TWO: HEAVEN

Verse 6: And God said, Let there be a firmament in the midst of the waters, and let it divide the waters from the waters.

According to verse 2, "... *And the Spirit of God moved upon the face of the waters,*" the water pre-existed. In verse 6, we read that God ordered an expanse in the middle of the waters to divide water from water. In verse 7, we read, "*And God made the firmament . . .*" Note the different uses of "create" and "made" as we move on in the study. He said it was good.

5

And God named the expanse which He had made HEAVEN; this took place on the second day. Just as surely as the "firmament" was formed by the Word of God, so are we: *"Being born again, not of corruptible seed, but of incorruptible, by the word of God, which liveth and abideth for ever" (I Peter 1:23).*

DAY THREE: EARTH AND PLANT LIFE

Verse 9: And God said, Let the waters under the heaven be gathered together unto one place, and let the dry land appear: and it was so.

The word "Let" or "allow" implies the Blessed Trinity at work in creation. In this work day, God gathered the waters together into one place under the sky (heaven) and He commanded that the dry land should appear and called it EARTH. The waters He named SEAS, and He saw that His work was good. We do not see the Creator "creating" on this day, but He was calling forth, and putting things already in existence into their place. God is a God of order.

Verse 11: And God said, Let the earth bring forth grass, the herb yielding seed, and the fruit tree yielding fruit after his kind, whose seed is in itself upon the earth: and it was so.

"Let the earth bring forth . . ." With heaven firmly fixed into its place, Elohim-God descended to this earth and decorated it for our living quarters. May we stress again that He is a God of order. So man was not to come forth until his home was ready. In these verses we have the BEGINNING of the law of the Harvest: each to produce after its own kind. He gave the earth and the seas the power to bring forth at His command and He said it was good.

6

DAY FOUR: MOON AND STARS

Verse 14: And God said, Let there be lights in the firmament of the heavens to divide the day from the night; and let them be for signs, and for seasons, and for days, and years:

Verse 15: And let them be for lights in the firmament of the heaven to give light upon the earth: and it was so.

Verse 16: And God made two great lights; the greater light to rule the day, and the lesser light to rule the night: he made the stars also.

This complemented day one. God took light already created, and He collected, fashioned and made it into several "luminaries" that all burst forth with majestic grandeur. God is the Father of light, and in Him there is no darkness. God set the moon, sun, and the stars in their places. The sun for the greater light (activity), and the moon to shine at night (rest). In this world we are "light bearers," and we are to let our light shine in the darkness of this sin-cursed earth, and He said it was good.

DAY FIVE: FISH AND FOWL

Verse 20: And God said, Let the waters bring forth abundantly the moving creature that hath life, and the fowl that may fly above the earth in the open firmament of heaven.

Verse 21: And God created great whales, and every living creature that moveth, which the waters brought forth abundantly, after their own kind, and every winged fowl after his own kind: and God saw that it was good.

In the above verse, we find that the literal translation for "whales" is "sea monsters." We also note that all things existed in groups that are interrelated. The further science advances, the more it is realized that all things are interconnected. One writer said that not only are the various orders of living things made according to their various minds, but even in inanimate nature there is amazing orderliness with infinite variety.

Just as the earth was commanded to bring forth in verse 11, the waters were told to bring forth abundantly in verse 20. Each after its own kind was commanded to be fruitful and to multiply. This fifth day complemented day two by filling the waters.

It was good.

DAY SIX: (1) ANIMAL KINGDOM

Verse 24: And God said, Let the earth bring forth the living creature after his own kind, cattle, and creeping thing, and beast of the earth after his kind: and it was so.

Verse 25: And God made the beast of the earth after his kind, and cattle after their kind, and every thing that creepeth upon the earth after his kind: and God saw that it was good.

Again the earth was commanded to bring forth. In verse 11, God said, *"Let the earth bring forth grass, the herb yielding seed, and the fruit tree yielding fruit..."* At that point the seed was within the earth ready to spring forth at the command of God; for had not the seasons and the light already been spoken into existence to aid the earth?

Now the earth was to bring forth living animals. This means God made them from the dust of the earth. The same dust particles from which He took man. He used existing materials. This day God filled the earth, which He had created on day three.

And it was good.

DAY SIX: (2) MAN

Verse 26: And God said, Let us make man in our image, after our likeness: and let them have dominion over the fish of the sea, and over the fowl of the air, and over the cattle, and over all the earth, and over every creeping thing that creepeth upon the earth.

Verse 27: So God created man in his own image, in the image of God created he him; male and female created he them.

FIRST DISPENSATION: INNOCENCE

FIRST COVENANT: EDENIC

Verse 28: And God blessed them, and God said unto them, Be fruitful, and multiply, and replenish the earth, and subdue it: and have dominion over the fish of the sea, and over the fowl of the air, and over every living thing that moveth upon the earth.

Verse 29: And God said, Behold, I have given you every herb bearing seed, which is upon the face of all the earth, and every tree, in the which is the fruit of a tree yielding seed; to you it shall be for meat.

9

Verse 30: And to every beast of the earth, and to every fowl of the air, and to every thing that creepeth upon the earth, wherein there is life, I have given every green herb for meat: and it was so.

Verse 31: And God saw every thing that he made, and behold, it was very good. And the evening and the morning were the sixth day.

It was all very good.

A dispensation is a period of time during which man is tested in respect to his obedience to some specific revelation of the will of God. Dispensations are a progressive and connected revelation of God's dealings with man, given sometimes to the whole race and at other times to a particular people, Israel. In each dispensation we view the grace of God, as He deals with man, to reconcile the world back to Himself. Dispensations are not different ways to salvation. Before the Cross, man was saved in prospect of Christ's atoning sacrifice, through believing the revelation thus far given to him. Since the Cross, man is saved by believing on Him in Whom revelation and redemption are consummated. Obedience to God remains the same in all dispensations. Thus, the purpose of dispensations is to place man under a specific rule of "conduct," all leading towards the coming of the Lord Jesus. There are seven dispensations:

(1) Innocence
(2) Conscience
(3) Human Government
(4) Promise
(5) Law
(6) Church
(7) Kingdom

Man was made the same day as the beast; their bodies were made of the same earth. Man was favored by God in every way, and put in an environment never equalled. He "created" and "formed" man. He would form his body from materials already in existence; but far more intricate and mind dazzling are the spirit and soul that God breathed into that newly formed clay.

IN THE IMAGE OF GOD

Man was made in the likeness and "image" of God on the sixth day of creation. Man was the reason for creation; All that Elohim-God brought forth by the Words of His Power, He gave to Adam and Eve. In the "image" of his creator was he created, bearing the marks of His "dignity and honor." In Adam we lost that "image," but in Christ all has been restored.

In Leviticus 19:17, we read that we are not to hate our brother, or rebuke him in any way: *"Thou shalt not hate they brother in thine heart: thou shalt in any wise rebuke they neighbor, and not suffer sin upon him. Thou shalt not avenge, nor bear any grudge against the children of thy people, but thou shalt love thy neighbour as thyself: I am the Lord."* This commandment must be remembered daily in light of the creation of man who was fashioned and formed in the "image" and "likeness" of God Himself, for we are told to respect each man's "dignity" and "honor," for he is made in the "perfection" of God. *"...I Am the Lord,"* might well read, *"You are not the Lord; I AM."*

DOMINION

"Behold," meaning "Look!" I have created it, and I have given it to you. When man was finished, God said *"It is very good."* The word "good" in the dictionary has the following meanings, which will add greatly to our understanding of the inheritance of Adam as lord of the earth:

(1) morally excellent
(2) satisfactory in quality
(3) good health
(4) honorable and worthy
(5) not counterfeit
(6) not spoiled or tainted
(7) skillfully or expertly done

God created man in His own "image" of "perfection," morally excellent; satisfactory in quality; in good health, honorable and worthy; unspoiled; and it was skillfully and expertly done. God then said, *"I REALLY DID A GOOD JOB!"* And He gave man dominion over the works of His hands; He kept nothing back from man.

At this point we must consider the number seven for it is God's number denoting "perfection" or "completeness." In the Hebrew there are just seven words in the opening verse of Genesis 1. They are composed of 28 letters, which is seven multiplied by four, and four is the number for "natural man" or "universal."

There are seven distinct stages in God's work of creation:

(1) The activity of the Holy Spirit 1:2
(2) Light 1:3
(3) Firmament (heaven)...................... 1:6-9
(4) Vegetation 1:11

(5) Arranging heavenly bodies 1:14-18
(6) Storing of waters 1:20-21
(7) Stocking of the earth 1:24

The word "made" is found seven times in this section:

(1) God made the firmament 1:7
(2) God made two great lights 1:16
(3) God made the beasts of the earth 1:25
(4) God said, Let us make man 1:26
(5) God saw everything that he had made 1:31
(6) God ended the work which he made 2:2
(7) God blessed ... sanctified ... rested ... from all his
     work which God created and made 2:3

The word "heaven" is mentioned seven times in chapter 1:

(1) In the beginning God created the heaven 1:1
(2) God called the firmament heaven 1:8
(3) ... Let the waters under the heaven 1:9
(4) ... Let there be lights in the firmament of
     heaven 1:14
(5) Let them be for lights in the firmament of
     the heaven 1:15
(6) God set them in the firmament of heaven ... 1:17
(7) ... Let waters bring forth ... in the open
     firmament of heaven 1:20

God Himself is mentioned in this 35 times, which is
seven multiplied by five. The number five denotes
"grace." Thus, we witness the seal of His perfection
stamped upon all He did and made and created.

There are seven great BEGINNINGS recorded in the
Book of Genesis. They comprise the sum of the things
more fully developed in the other books of the Bible:

(1) The beginning of the universe, the heavens
     and earth
(2) The beginning of the human race
(3) The beginning of sin
(4) The beginning of redemption
(5) The beginning of nations
(6) The beginning of the Hebrew race
(7) The beginning of the life of faith

2. THE FIRST REST
(Genesis 2)

DAY SEVEN: SABBATH

Verse 1: Thus the heavens and the earth were finished, and all the host of them.

Verse 2: And on the seventh day God ended his work which he had made; and he rested on the seventh day from all his work which he had made.

Verse 3: And God blessed the seventh day, and sanctified it: because that in it he had rested from all his work which God created and made.

The day of rest has a far deeper meaning than what we can cover at this point. He rested and He gave a day of rest to man; a time when man could come aside for unbroken fellowship with Him, and for the development of closer family ties.

Sabbath comes from the Hebrew word *"Shabbat"* meaning "rest." The Sabbath day was instituted as a memorial to God's creation. Man has his own special ways of polluting God's simple instructions, and the gift from God soon became a burden instead of a delight by the institution of "religious" ceremonies.

God "desisted" from His work indicating that nothing could be added or subtracted to His masterpiece. So perfect is His love and care for us, we find our fulfillment in type in this "rest" in Jesus, Who is our *"Shabbat."*

Verse 4: These are the generations of the heavens and of the earth when they were created, in the day that the Lord God made the earth and the heavens.

Verse 5: And every plant of the field before it was in the earth, and every herb of the field before it grew: for the Lord God had not caused it to rain upon the earth, and there was not a man to till the ground.

Verse 6: But there went up a mist from the earth, and watered the whole of the face of the ground.

In order to follow the story without interruption, we must note that chapter two is a more detailed account of what we have already studied. In verse one and two it tells of the "rest" of God. This detailed account of God's six days of work revealed that God had held back the rains until the appointed time when He would place man in the garden of Eden. For instance, the plants and herbs of the field had been spoken into existence, but they were still in the earth until the sixth day. Faith-empowered Words had created them, but they had not sprouted.

Verse 7: And God formed man of the dust of the ground, and breathed into his nostrils the breath of life; and man became a living soul.

The blood covenant began in the garden. God breathed the breath of life into Adam (Hebrew-Adham), meaning "Red" or "Ruddy" or "earth bound," and man became a living soul. He was born in the "image" of His Creator. God breathed . . . breath is Spirit; He breathed the breath of life. . . (spirit) into that lump of clay, and man became a "thing alive!" With the dust of the ground He formed his body: by His Own spirit He breathed spirit into man; and by creation man became a living soul. The instant that God breathed the breath of life into Adham, blood flowed into his veins. In Leviticus 17:11 and 14, we read, *"For the*

15

life of the flesh is in the blood . . ." *"For it is the life of all flesh; the blood . . ."* It was the blood of God that began to pump into Adam's heart.

In the book of Exodus, God told Moses His Covenant Name. Then He said, *"Now shalt thou see what I will do to Pharaoh; for with a strong hand shall he let them go, and with a strong hand shall he drive them out of his land. And God spake unto Moses, and said unto him, I am the Lord: and I appeared unto Abraham, and Isaac, and Jacob, by the Name of God Almighty, but by my Name Jehovah (Yahweh) was I not known to them. And I have also established my covenant with them . . ." (Exodus 6:1-4).*

He revealed Himself to Moses as a covenant keeping God before He sent him into Pharaoh's courts. In Genesis 2, we find Moses using one of the Names of God not known during the days of the Patriarchs. *"Yahweh God made . . ."* or *"And Yahweh formed man . . ."* He was nevertheless, a covenant God, who had breathed the breath of life into Adam.

FIRST COVENANT: EDENIC

GARDEN OF EDEN (DELIGHT)

Verse 8: And the Lord God planted a garden eastward in Eden; and there he put the man whom he had formed.

Verse 9: And out of the ground made the Lord God to grow every tree that is pleasant to the sight, and good for food; the tree of life also in the midst of the garden, and the tree of the knowledge of good and evil.

Eastward of Eden, God planted a garden; Adam had full authority to name all the animals, and care for the trees and plants. He was master of all he surveyed. His home was furnished and garnished by nature's beauty. He would keep the garden without toil or labor; but when he fell and cried out, *"I was afraid,"* he was like one in a cold sweat. Extreme and extended fears can cause the body to pour sweat from the veins in an abnormal way. In the garden, Jesus sweat as it were, great drops of blood as He fought our battles.

In the book of Revelation we are told of the "city-four-square" that is being prepared for us. This will be paradise regained. *"And I saw a new heaven and a new earth: for the first heaven and the first earth were passed away; and there was no more sea . . . the holy city, new Jerusalem, coming down from God out of heaven, prepared as a bride adorned for her husband . . . the tabernacle of God is with men, and God himself shall be with them, and be their God . . . Behold, I make all things new . . . And the city had no need of the sun, neither of the moon, to shine in it: for the glory of God did lighten it, and the Lamb is the light thereof . . ." (Revelation 21).*

"The tree of life . . . the tree of knowledge of good and evil:" Two trees in the garden were especially pointed out to Adam, and he was given a commandment. He had life, but his life was only his by virtue of submission to the revealed will of God, his Creator.

In the garden of Eden could be found every provision for man's spirit, soul, and body. He was living in the height of prosperity and beauty. What artist, however accomplished, could do justice to that opening scene of time when God led Adam by the hand and placed him in the garden that He Himself had prepared? The Master Artist had stepped out of eternity and breathed multiple colors of softest hues upon His canvas of white, and thus created a masterpiece unequalled to man, and He handed it all to Adam. *"See what I did just for you, Adam!"*

The tree of life was no doubt a sign and symbol to Adam of his eternal life upon the earth. He could look upon that particular tree and be reminded of God's grace and favor towards him; like God, a life without end.

Let us turn our attention from the tree of life to the tree of knowledge of good and evil, which was also in the midst of the garden and was a symbol to Adam. Adam had been fashioned in a state of "innocence," and he would have to be tested.

This tree was forever a reminder to us that as far back as the garden, God has written a law upon the hearts of all men: *"Do this and live — disobey, and you will surely die."* This tree was planted by God; but there was a second tree planted on Calvary hill by the wicked hands of man.

FOUR RIVERS

Verse 10: And a river went out of Eden to water the garden; and from thence it was parted, and became into four heads. This river branched out into four heads (streams), reminding us that what God plants, He will water. The Pishon river is lost to us. It was the river which compassed the whole land of Havilah, where there was gold. The name of the

18

second river was Gihon, and it compassed the whole land of Cush (Ethiopia). This river is also lost to us. The third river was Hiddekel, and it flowed towards the east of Assyria (Asshur). And the fourth River is the Euphrates. In the book of Revelation we see the four heads coming together as a "pure river of life," with the tree of life restored to us. *"And He showed me a pure river of water of life, clear as crystal, proceeding out of the throne of God and of the Lamb. In the midst of it, and on either side of the river, was there the tree of life, which bare twelve manner of fruits, and yielded her fruit every month: and the leaves of the tree were for the healing of the nations" (Revelation 22:1-2).*

THE FIRST BRIDE

Verse 18: And the Lord God said, It is not good that man should be alone; I will make him an help meet for him.

Verse 19: And out of the ground the Lord God formed every beast of the field, and every fowl of the air; and brought them unto Adam to see what he would call them: and whatsoever Adam called every living creature, that was the name thereof.

Verse 20: And Adam gave names to all cattle, and to the fowl of the air, and to every beast of the field; but for Adam there was not found a help meet for him.

Verse 21: And God caused a deep sleep to fall upon Adam, and he slept: and he took one of his ribs, and closed up the flesh instead thereof:

Verse 22: And the rib, which the Lord God had taken from man, made he a woman, and brought her unto the man.

3. THE FALL OF MAN
(Genesis 3)

Man was created male and female according to the Word of God. Then the woman was taken out of man's side, and given her own identity. This is the "beginning" of marriage and the family ties. The strength of family bonds defies any kind of clear-cut explanation on the natural plane. This is also a part of the "blood covenant," as far as our relationship to God and to our kin. The love and loyalty God established between families began when He took Eve from Adam's own flesh and bone and blood. In other words, Adam's blood was now her blood.

The Hebrew translation for the word "rib" comes from a root word meaning "cell," which also can be defined as "cage" in which something is contained. In the human body we know that every single cell contains all the necessary ingredients to form the exact duplication of "another" in kind: a likeness. Adam contained in his person, at first, all the "cells" that were yet to form the entire human race. So when he fell, the entire human race went with him.

Eve (mother of all living) is a type of the church (bride) born from the side of our Lord Jesus Christ as He hung on the TREE. In John 19:34, we read, *"But one of the soldiers with a spear pierced his side, and forthwith came there out blood and water."* That blood and water should flow from the side of one already dead was indeed a miracle. The water and the blood served as God's witness of His Son and of the life sinners may find through His shed Blood.

The action of the soldier on that day was symbolic of the enmity God had set forth as a result of the fall of man. One writer stated it was the sullen shot of the defeated enemy after the battle . In type, Jesus now became the sleeping last Adam, and out of His side was formed the evangelical Eve. Behold, the Rock which was smitten, and the waters of life gushed forth. Behold, the fountain that is opened for sin and uncleanness. "The blood and water signified the two great benefits which all believers partake of through Christ, (1) justification, (2) santification; blood stands for remission, and water for regeneration; blood for atonement, water for purification. The two must always go together" stated Matthew Henry.

THE SERPENT

Verse 1: Now the serpent was more subtle than any beast of the field which the Lord had made. And he said unto the woman, Yea, hath God said, Ye shall not eat of every tree of the garden?

Verse 2: And the woman said unto the serpent, We may eat of the fruit of the trees of the garden:

Verse 3: But of the fruit of the tree which is in the midst of the garden, God hath said, Ye shall not eat of it, neither shall ye touch it, lest ye die.

Verse 4: And the serpent said unto the woman, Ye shall not surely die;

Verse 5: For God doth know that in the day ye eat thereof, then your eyes shall be opened, and ye shall be as gods, knowing good and evil.

God's first covenant was made with Adam; His gift to them was the "garden of delight" and total dominion of the entire earth. As a covenant-keeping God, when man fell, He could not prove unfaithful to

His Word, for He was bound by His Blood flowing through our first parents.

We must be willing to trust God's purpose and plan for mankind as we read of the temptation and utter ruin of man. The serpent was the medium (tool) through which Satan (fallen Lucifer) operated to deceive. He was not the despicable, loathsome creature we see today.

The problem of the origin of evil is pre-historic. No one can claim total knowledge along these lines. The answer ís not easy and is simply ignored by most who view God as a God of perfection and total love. However, certain scriptures seem to loom before us that either have to be dealt with or skipped over in light of the lack of total knowledge. Certain passages do not seem to harmonize with the His mercy and favor. Space will not allow us to delve into the many theories, but allow only for suggestion of certain scriptures to be studies in light of the absolute sovereignty of Almighty God to handle the affairs of man. In Isaiah 45:5-10, we read, *"I am the Lord, and there is none else, there is no God beside me: I girded thee, though thou hast not known me. That they may know from the rising of the sun, and from the west, that there is none beside me. I am the Lord, and there is none else. I form the light, and create darkness: I make peace, and create evil: I the Lord do all these things. Drop down, ye heavens, from above, and let the skies pour down righteousness: let the earth open, and let them bring forth salvation, and let righteousness spring up together; I the Lord have created it. Woe unto him that striveth with his Maker! Let the potsherd strive with the potsherds of the earth. Shall the clay say to him that fashioneth it, What makest thou? or they work, He hath no hands? Woe unto him that saith unto his father, What begettest thou? or to the woman, What hast thou brought forth?"* Through the entire chapter God is declaring His sovereign reign, and that there is no other God beside Him. He can call a man by his name, even though the man has never called upon the Lord. He has promised strength and victory to those who are obedient to His call. He formed the light, and He made the darkness; He said that he sends the good times and He sends the bad times. Woe to anyone who fights against his Creator.

In Isaiah 54:15-17, we have the assurance that the evil that has been created, will never be used against the righteous. Evil in this world is the result of disobedience. Satan is the deceiver, and he whispers to the hearts of the untrained that God is punishing them for their sins. It is a lie. It is full of subtlety and deception; it is a cave full of dead men's bones. God answers that for us in His Word, *"Behold, they shall surely gather together, but not by me: whosoever shall gather together against thee shall fall for thy sake. Behold, I have created the smith that bloweth the coals in the fire, and that bringeth forth an instrument for his work; and I have created the waster to destroy. No weapon formed against thee shall prosper; and every tongue that shall rise against thee in judgment thou shalt condemn. This is the heritage of the servants of the Lord, and their righteousness is of me, saith the Lord."* Is it not clear that God has the final say? He assured us that when the devil gathers his forces against us, it is not of Him. Sickness, bruises, and sorrows are not of God. He clearly stated that He Himself formed the waster to destroy the wicked. The devil will be cast into the lake of fire in the end. God promised that the enemy would fall for our sake. No weapon that is formed or fashioned in the fires of the blacksmith will prevail against us. We have the protection of the Lord. The weapons are for those who disobeyed the Will of God; for those who refuse to receive His Son as their Saviour and Lord. He is not mad at His children. He will use those weapons to destroy our enemies, just as surely as he gave the city of Jericho to Joshua in his day.

Verse 6: And the woman saw that the tree was good for food, and that it was pleasant to the eyes, and a tree to be desired to make one wise, she took of the fruit thereof, and did eat, and gave also unto her husband with her; and he did eat.

SECOND DISPENSATION: CONSCIENCE

SECOND COVENANT: ADAMIC

Verse 7: And the eyes of them both were opened, and they knew that they were naked; and they sewed fig leaves together, and made themselves aprons.

THE SERPENT

The serpent was the vehicle through which Satan operated. Man up to that time was neither moral or immoral; among all the beasts of the field and animals that Adam had named, the serpent was the most beautiful and colorful. He did not have to slip into the garden: he was a part of the Edenic scene. It is totally misleading to teach that by some devious means he had to approach Eve. He lived around them. *"Serpent, your name is deception: Satan, you are the instigator of it all!"*

We must consider at this point the fact that the serpent talked. He carried on a conversation with Eve; this was no figment of her imagination or just a suggestion that came to her mind. It was not unusual for Adam and Eve to love and fellowship with the animals God had created. Allow at this point a quote from Josephus, the Jewish historian, "God, therefore, commanded that Adam and his wife should eat of all the rest of the plants, but to abstain from the tree of knowledge; and foretold them that, if they touched it, it would prove their destruction. But while all the living creatures had one language, all that time the serpent, which then lived together with Adam and his wife, shewed an envious disposition, at his supposal of their living happily and in obedience to the commands of God; and imagining that when they disobeyed them, they would fall into calamities, he persuaded the woman, out of a malicious intention, to taste of the tree of knowledge, telling them that in that tree was the knowledge of good and evil; which knowledge when they should obtain, they would lead a happy life, nay, a life not inferior to that of a god; by which means he overcame the woman, and persuaded her to despise the command of God. Now when she had tasted of the tree, and was pleased with its fruit, she persuaded Adam to make use of it also, . . . and thereby brought him in a calamitous condition. He also deprived the serpent of speech, out of indignation at his malicious disposition towards Adam. Beside this, he inserted a poison under his tongue and made him an enemy to men."

One must not be dogmatic in cases of limited revelation regarding certain truths and passages of scriptures. God holds within His Own heavenly files many answers that will be revealed only when we behold His Face; but we know that God did not tempt Adam and Eve to sin. He tested their trust in Him; His command could not have been spelled out any more clearly. It remains true today that sin brings heartache.

With the possible exception of the birth and ministry of our Lord Jesus Christ, this is the most important chapter in the entire Bible. Man was free to exercise his own will; he did just that, then blamed the results upon God who created him.

By obedience to the command of God, man could have had an endless life in the garden. Let us be assured that since God is both omniscient and omnipotent, He was not astonished by the outbreak of Satan. We cannot harmonize the story of creation and the battle of Armageddon, unless we believe that Satan has always had to work within the limits and boundaries of the eternal plan of God. He did not wait until a Redeemer was needed to provide One. *"And all that dwell upon the earth shall worship him, whose names are not written in the book of life of the Lamb slain from the foundation of the world" (Revelation 13:8):*

This describes the end-time upheaval where Satan is having his last fling with the saints of God. He blasphemed God, His Name, the Temple, and all those in heaven. For a time he is given great power, and all whose names are not written in the Lamb's book of life will be deceived, and worship him (Anti-Christ). May we add one more thought to the omnipotence of our God? In Acts 15:18, we read, *"Known unto God are all his works from the beginning of the world."*

Let us view this situation with these four points in mind: (1) God had given them the promise (covenant), but it was not unconditional; (2) a precept was involved: the command of *"Do not eat of the tree of knowledge of good and evil."* (3) aspect of this situation was the test: will you obey me, or will you listen to the enemy when he misquotes My Word and tempts you? (4) God offered them a paradise, but He was ready with the provision when they fell.

Freedom means we have a choice. Man was free to choose. God endowed man with a soul and therein lies man's ability to chose the right from the wrong. He has never been innocent regarding the results of sinning against God. The evil was in the disobedience to the direct command of God, the "precept."

4. THE WAY OF CAIN (GOTTEN)
(Genesis 4)   (3971 B.C.)

In this chapter we have the history of the first civilization. According to the Chronological Bible the date of the garden was 3975 B.C., and the birth of Cain was 3972 B.C. Then one year later, Abel (ascends) was born. At the birth of Cain, Eve declared "... *I have gotten a man from the Lord.*" One translation reads, "*I have gotten a Man, even Yahweh!*"

Verse 2: And she again bare his brother Abel. And Abel was a keeper of sheep, but Cain was a tiller of the ground.

Verse: And the process of time it came to pass, that Cain brought of the fruit of the ground an offering unto the Lord.

Verse 4: And Abel, he also brought of the firstlings of his flock and of the fat thereof. And the Lord had respect unto Abel and to his offering:

Verse 5: But unto Cain and to his offering he had not respect. And Cain was very wroth, and his countenance fell.

The central theme set before us is worship. God has always revealed His ways to man. There are three things to be considered about these offerings: (1) There was a definite place where God would be worshipped. The firstling and the fat are suggestive of an altar where the victim was offered and the fat burned, (2) God had provided a definite time, (in the process of time), and (3) God Himself had provided the means of worship: it was to be a blood sacrifice, and nothing else would please Him. He did not respect Cain's offering because he had violated the principles set down by God regarding sacrifices. His attitude was clearly denounced by God. Abel offered his sacrifice by faith. In Hebrews 11:4, we read, *"By faith Abel offered unto God a more excellent sacrifice than Cain, by which he obtained witness that he was righteous, God testifying of his gifts: and by it he being dead yet speaketh."*

Also, we should consider the three principles involved if the sacrifice offered up was to be accepted: (1) It must be God's gift, and His work alone, (2) It must be the death of an innocent substitute with no blemish, and (3) It must be by the shedding of innocent blood; for the life of the flesh is in the blood. It is most likely the offerings were even then accepted by fire as recorded in Leviticus 9:24 *"And there came a fire out from before the Lord, and consumed upon the altar the burnt offering and the fat: which when all the people saw, they shouted, and fell on their faces."*

Cain was a type of the religious man of this world; Abel in type was the spiritual man who sought the things of God. In Cain we have three things to list: (1) First false religion, (2) First murder, (3) First Man God cursed. Cain foreshadowed man's feeble attempt to come to God in his own way which is by works and not by faith.

Verse 6: And the Lord said unto Cain, Why art thou wroth? And why is thy countenance fallen?

Verse 7: If thou doest well, shalt thou not be accepted? And if thou doest not well, sin lieth at the door: and unto thee shall be his desire, and thou shalt rule over him.

In the garden of Eden it was God who called out Adam, and talked with him about his sin; again, He took the initiative to seek out man and give him a chance to make things right. Whether fig leaves or fruit of the ground, God will not accept the works of man's hands. In other words, a bloodless sacrifice will not be accepted. While Cain was in the midst of his pity-party, God began to reason with him. He told him everything would be all right if he would obey and offer the sacrifice He required; with that came the ultimatum. Satan had entered the heart of Cain, and pride caused him to fall. God gave Cain a chance to rule over sin; He told him if he persisted in this disobedience, sin would attack him and rule him all his life.

Verse 8: *And Cain talked with Abel his brother: and it came to pass, when they were in the field, that Cain rose up against Abel his brother, and slew him.*

Cain could not get "at God" so he struck out at his own brother. In I John 3:11-12, we are warned where evil works can lead: *"For this is the message that ye heard from the beginning, that we should love one another. Not as Cain, who was of that wicked one, and slew his brother. And wherefore slew he him? Because his own works were evil, and his brother's righteous."* In Jude 11, another warning is sounded out about the way of Cain, *"Woe unto them! for they have gone the way of Cain, and ran greedily after the error of Balaam for reward, and perished in the gain-saying of Core."*

Cain not only killed his brother, but he lied to God. Sin cannot be hid; yet how depraved the human heart when it can look into the Holy Eyes of God and lie.

Verse 9: And the Lord said unto Cain, Where is Abel thy brother? And he said, I know not: Am I my brother's keeper?

Since he had refused to make his sacrifices right, became angry with God, murdered his brother, then lied to God, the Lord could no longer deal with him in mercy. Judgment was his lot. God told Cain, *"The voice of your brother's blood cries out vengence unto me."* (When Jesus shed His Blood, the cry was one of Mercy). Cain was cursed from the place where he had shed innocent blood upon the ground.

He was told his toil would be hard and the crops would often fail. He would be branded as a fugitive every where he wandered.

Cain was like the religious leaders in the day of Jesus who cried, *"His blood be on us, and on our children" (Matthew 27: 25).* But the Blood of Jesus *". . . speaketh better things than that of Abel" (Hebrews 12: 24).* Cain went forth complaining that his punishment was too great, and that every one would try to kill him. God set a mark upon Cain. We are not to spend time speculating about this mark, but God would give anyone guilty of slaying Cain seven times the punishment He had assigned to wicked Cain.

Cain and his wife went to live in the land of Nod (wandering), east of Eden, and there they had a son named Enoch. (This is not the Enoch who walked

31

with God.) The question of where Cain got his wife is quite simple. He married either a sister or a niece. In that first generation of multiplication upon the earth, all of Adam's sons had to marry one of their sisters. One commentary states that Adam had three sons, and 29 daughters. In that early time, there were no mutant genes in the genetic systems of any of the offspring, so that meant no genetic harm could have resulted from close marriages.

CAIN
  ENOCH (dedication)
   IRAD (wild ass)
    MEHUJAEL (God is combating)
     METHUSAEL (man of God)
      LAMECH (overthrower)

Lamech took unto himself two wives, (the beginning of polygamy). One was named Adah, (ornament), and the other was Zillah (shade). Adah had a son named Jabal who was the father of tents and cattle. In the east when one was said to be the "father" of something, that meant he was the originator. His brother was Jubal, the first musician and inventor of the harp and flute.

The other wife, Zillah, had Tubal-cain. He was a maker of the first weapons, working with bronze and iron metals. Lamech displayed the height of arrogance when he confessed to his wives how he had murdered two men for just bruising him. He bragged about his ability to use the weapons of war; he sang out that God had promised to avenge Cain, who had no weapons, seven-fold, but he was greater for he could avenge himself seventy-fold with his weapons.

This tragically reflects the total depravity of his character, and mirrors the spirit of his age.

Verse 25: And Adam knew his wife again; and she bare a son, and called his name Seth: For God, said she, hath appointed me another seed instead of Abel, whom Cain slew.

By now Adam had been on the earth about 130 years; there is the possibility that close to 500,000 people were scattered across the land. He lived 800 more years and begat sons and daughters. Adam was contemporary with all of Cain and Seth's posterity down to the 308th year of Enoch, and 243 years of Methuselah (950 years total). So the story of the fall was told firsthand for quite some time.

5. ENOCH
(Genesis 5)   (2988 B.C.)

TRANSLATED BY FAITH

This is the book of the generations of Adam. It marks one of the major divisions of Genesis. In this verse we read, *"This is the book of the generations of Adam . . ."* In the New Testament we read in Matthew 1:1, *". . . the book of the generations of Jesus Christ."*

Verse 3: And Adam lived a hundred and thirty years, and begat a son in his own likeness, after his image; and called his name Seth:

NAME:	DEATH	MEANING
SETH	905 Years	(appointed)
ENOS		(frailty)
CAINAN	910 Years	(acquisition)
MAHALALEEL	895 Years	(God be praised)
JARED	962 Years	(descent)
METHUSELAH	969 Years	(when he dies, judgment)
LAMECH	777 Years	(conqueror)
NOAH	950 Years	(rest)

Approximately 1,656 years have past since the creation story. When the meanings of names are given, they will vary in many cases, just as the exact years cannot be absolute. This list of names is repeated in I Chronicles 1:1-4 and Luke 3:36-38.

Verse 21: And Enoch lived sixty and five years, and begat Methuselah:

Verse 22: And Enoch walked with God after be begat Methuselah three hundred years, and begat sons and daughters:

Verse 23: And all the days of Enoch were three hundred sixty and five years:

Verse 24: And Enoch walked with God: and he was not; for God took him.

Enoch maintained a close relationship with God, *"By faith Enoch was translated that he should not see death, and was not found, because God had translated him" (Hebrews 11:5).*

Centuries later the prophet Elijah was similarly taken into heaven without tasting death (II Kings 2:11). One writer noted that Enoch prophesied about midway between Adam and Abraham, and Elijah about midway between Abraham and Christ, and both lived and ministered during times of deep apostasy.

Methuselah (when he dies it will come), signified by his name, that the flood would not come upon the earth until his death. He lived 969 years, and lived longer than any of the other men in recorded history. His son, Lamech, was the father of Noah.

Enoch is a type of those saints who are to be translated before the apocalyptic judgements (Revelation).

6. NOAH
(Genesis 6)

In the fifth chapter of Genesis we have the ten generations from Adam to Noah, covering more than 1650 years. Adam was still living when Noah's father, Lamech, was born, and he lived fifty years thereafter. He lived to retell his tragic story of disobedience in the garden of Eden to a long line of ancestry. Noah (comfort and rest) was the first man born after the death of Adam, and his birth became the heralding of a new age for mankind. He had a good spiritual background since he was the great grandson of Methuselah, and the great-great grandson of Enoch. He served as the connecting link between . . . *"the world that then was, being overflowed with water: But the heavens and the earth, which are now, by the same word are kept in store, reserved unto fire against the day of judgment and perdition of ungodly men" (II Peter 3:6-7).*

WORLD CONDITIONS

Sin was spreading like leprosy. It infiltrated first a family, then a whole society. It was universal apostasy; the total abandonment of the principles and commands of God. Since Cain's posterity had no true beliefs to abandon, it was Seth's line that apostatized.

Verse 1: And it came to pass, when men began to multiply on the face of the earth, and daughters were born unto them,

Verse 2: That the sons of God saw the daughters of men that were fair; and they took them wives of all which they chose.

Verse 3: And the Lord said, My spirit shall not always strive with man, for he also is flesh: yet his days shall be an hundred and twenty years.

Verse 4: There were giants in the earth in those days; and after that, when the sons of God came unto the daughters of men, and they bare children to them, the same became mighty men, which were of old, men of renown.

The sons of the Sethites saw the daughters of men who were the Cainites, and they married into this ungodly line. This was Satan's attempt to corrupt the pure bloodline through which the Lamb of God would come. Spiritual decline is inevitable when God's people begin to compromise. God is righteous and must judge. In Amos 3:3, we read, *"Can two walk together, except they be agreed?"* In II Corinthians 6:14-16, the Apostle Paul sounds the same warning to believers, *"Be ye not unequally yoked together with unbelievers: for what fellowship hath righteousness with unrighteousness? and what communion hath light with darkness? And what concord hath Christ with Belial? Or what part hath he that believeth with an infidel? And what agreement hath the temple of God with idols? For ye are the temple of the living God; as God hath said, I will dwell in them and walk in them; and I will be their God, and they shall be my people."*

In verse four of our text, we read, *"There were giants in the earth . . ."* The word "giants" in the Hebrew is *"Nephilim,"* and does not mean the same as our English word for giants. Every Hebrew word has a root meaning, and the root in this word is from the meaning "fell" or "fallen" thus, this would mean that there were fallen ones in the earth. Only to Adam and his offspring was the command given to be fruitful and multiply and fill the earth. This command was never given to angels, who are neither godly nor ungodly. They do not have the capability to reproduce. This intermarriage resulted in the whole world being full of sin and spiritual disease. These ungodly unions caused the whole world to be filled with diseases and wickedness. Mighty men, when taken from Hebrew, means hero or champion.

Verse 5: And God saw that the wickedness of man was great in the earth, and that every imagination of the thoughts of his heart was only evil continually.

Verse 6: And it repented the Lord that he had made man on the earth, and it grieved him at his heart.

Verse 7: And the Lord said, I will destroy man whom I have created from the face of the earth; both man, and beast, and the creeping thing, and the fowls of the air; for it repenteth me that I have made them.

Verse 8: But Noah found grace in the eyes of the Lord.

Verse 9: These are the generations of Noah: Noah was a just man and perfect in his generation, and Noah walked with God.

Verse 10: And Noah begat three sons, Shem, Ham, and Japheth.

Verse 11: The earth also was corrupt before God, and the earth was filled with violence.

Verse 12: And God looked upon the earth, and behold, it was corrupt; for all flesh had corrupted his way upon the earth.

Verse 13: And God said unto Noah, The end of all flesh is come before me; for the earth is filled with violence through them; and, behold I will destroy them with the earth.

But Noah found grace in the eyes of the Lord in the midst of violence and total depravity. Grace is the foundation of every life that is well-pleasing to God. One writer said that grace is the source from which issues every blessing we receive. It was the grace of God and not the graces of Noah which preserved him from a watery grave. This is the first time in our study that the word "grace" has appeared. It is to be noted that man had fallen to the lowest pit, and Grace, magnificent Grace, came to bridge the gap between man and God. Noah lived in a time when man could do no more or fall any lower. He was a preacher of righteousness.

Man began to multiply upon the face of the earth. This was the effect of the blessing; yet man proved to be so depraved that the blessings turned into a curse.

In Genesis 6:9, we have described for us the character of Noah. Noah was a just man. He was a perfect man in his generation; and he walked with God. In Hebrews 11:7 we read of the faith of Noah: *"By faith Noah, being warned of God of things not seen as yet, moved with fear, prepared an ark to the saving of his house; by which he commanded the world, and became heir of the righteousness which is by faith."* Noah knew the voice of God, and he was quick to obey. He rested his faith upon the Word of God in the midst of a world flooded with men living after the dictates of their own evil flesh.

THE ARK

Verse 14: Make thee an ark of gopher wood; rooms shalt thou make in the ark, and shalt pitch it within and without with pitch.

Verse 15: And this is the fashion which thou shalt make it of: The length of the ark shall be three hundred cubits, the breadth of it fifty cubits, and the height of it thirty cubits.

Verse 16: A window shalt thou make to the ark, and in a cubit shalt thou finish it above: and the door of the ark shalt thou set in the side thereof; with lower, second, and third stories shalt thou make it.

This ark was a type of Christ as our Ark of Safety in the earth today. It was "divine provision" for Noah and his family during the deluge. Before Noah needed an ark, God had begun to prepare it for him. A Sovereign God will look ahead and prepare for His own.

Next, we take note of the fact that God revealed His plans to Noah before He made a move in any direction. Today God reveals His secrets to us by the Holy Spirit. In Amos 3:7 we read, *"Surely, the Lord God will do nothing but he revealeth his secret unto his servants the prophets."*

The ark was not the idea of Noah; it was the Divine Plan of an Almighty God to get His Son into the earth. The devil is ever behind the scenes trying to thwart the plans of the Lord.

The ark was to be made of gopher wood, which typifies the humanity of our Lord Jesus Christ, who was *". . . a root out of a dry ground" (Isaiah 53:2).*

There are three arks mentioned in the Word of God, and each time they are foreshadowing the refuge that Jesus gives to all believers who trust in Him. We have the ark of Noah; the ark of bulrushes in Exodus 2:3, which protected Moses from the murderous designs of Pharaoh, who was a type of Satan. Then we have the ark of the covenant which sheltered the two tables of stone on which were inscribed the Holy law of God.

Man was invited to come into this ark, (Genesis 7:1). In Acts 4:12, we read, *"Neither is there salvation in any other; for there is none other name under heaven given among men, whereby we must be saved."* The invitation remains the same as when God said to Noah, *"Come thou and all thy house into the ark,"* for it was not a command but a gentle invitation.

The ark was lined with pitch within and without. No matter how high the waters rose, its passengers were securely nestled within. This ark was about the size of a modern day ocean liner. It was a three-storied ship with lots of rooms and stalls. It was 450 feet in length, 75 feet wide, and 45 feet high. It carried eight grown people and possibility 7000 different species of animals. Neither the people nor the animals were allowed to reproduce during that time.

The ark had one door. the tabernacle in the wilderness had only one door. Jesus said, *"I am the*

41

door" (John 10:9). Noah was told to set the door in the side of the ark. Surely this speaks, in type, of the piercing of our Lord's side in John 19:34.

An ark with three stories? One might wonder why we are told how many stories to this ark. Since the ark unmistakably foreshadowed the Lord Jesus Christ, it would speak to us of our three-fold salvation; it is a salvation which embraces the spirit, soul, and body. Also, we have a three tense salvation: we have been saved from the penalty of sin; we are being saved from its power; we shall yet be saved and delivered from the presence of sin. Still another thought to be considered is that we worship a triune Godhead: Father, Son, and Holy Spirit and in that order. We worship the Father in the Name of the Son by the power of the Holy Spirit.

Next we observe that the window was not to be below but above. Noah and his family were not to be looking around at the high waters of their circumstances, but they were to keep looking up towards God. We will not press the issue of the many rooms (stalls), but move on to the blessed truth of atonement typically presented by the word "pitch" (Genesis 6:14). Scholars tells us that the Hebrew word here is not the common one for "pitch," which is "zetteth," but is "kapher," which is translated seventy times in the Old Testament as "to make atonement." The simple meaning of "kapher" is "to cover" and no where else is it rendered "pitch." Thus, we read that the ark was covered with the Blood of Jesus inside and out. As others have pointed out, the typical teaching of the ark reaches beyond the truth of "atonement" to "resurrection" itself, for the day the ark rested on Mount Ararat coincided with the day Jesus rose from the dead. It rested on the seventh day of the seventh month. However, by the commandment of the Lord, given at the time of the institution of the feast of the Passover, the seventh month was changed into the first month. Three days after the Passover, which was on the fourteenth day of the month, the Lord having passed through the waters of judgment, stood in resurrection in the midst of His disciples, saying, *"Peace be unto you" (John 20:21).*

In Psalm 91, Moses sang of the "Ark of Safety," that would house all of God's children who abide in Him. Comfort and rest were offered to those who trusted in His Divine protection. Christians are not to be afraid of the high waters of life; the ark of God shelters the inner life as well as the outward life. When we enter into the "ark," God shuts the door against the enemy of our soul, and there we are just as supernaturally safe from the outside forces, as Noah and his family were from the deluge.

7. THE FLOOD
(Genesis 7)   (2319 B.C.)

Verse 1: And the Lord said unto Noah, Come thou and all thy house into the ark; for thee have I seen righteous before me in this generation.

Verse 2: Of every clean beast thou shalt take to thee by sevens, and the male and his female: and of beasts that are not clean by two, the male and his female.

Verse 3: Of fowls also of the air by sevens, the male and the female; to keep seed alive upon the face of all the earth.

We note that Noah was told to take seven pairs of every clean beast, and of the unclean animals, he was instructed to take only two pairs. Here, God established a difference between clean and unclean, holy and unholy, righteous and the unrighteous. Only the pure, clean animals could be used for sacrifice. Another miracle of God was how Noah would have known which of the animals were the clean and which ones were the unclean. This, along with getting the animals into the ark in seven days, would have been the work of the angels and the Holy Spirit.

Verse 4: For yet seven days, and I will cause it to rain upon the earth forty days and forty nights; and every living substance that I have made will I destroy from off the face of the earth.

Verse 5: And Noah did according unto all that the Lord commanded him.

In Bible numerology forty is testing or probation period. Eight stands for new order or a new beginning. A Godly man with his family went into the ark (8) and it rained forty days and forty nights to cleanse the earth.

Verse 10: And it came to pass after seven days, that the waters of the flood were upon the earth.

Verse 11: In the six hundredth year of Noah's light, in the second month, and seventeenth day of the month, the same day were all the fountains of the great deep broken up, and the windows of heaven were opened.

Seven days before it began to rain, Noah went into the ark. It began to rain on the 17th day of the second month of his 600th year; for forty days waters prevailed. The windows of heaven opened up and drenched the earth. The fountains of the great deep broke up and joined the flood gates of heaven. This was more than just a flood. Waters above the ground and waters below once again united for destruction. All life upon the earth died. The waters prevailed for 150 days (or five months). Every thing was covered with water. Everything that had breath in its nostrils died in this flood. The ark then rested on the 17th day of the seventh month. The mountains became visible on the first day of the tenth month; they removed the covering of the ark on the first day of the first month of Noah's 601st year; he went out of the ark on the 27th day of the second month. He had been in the ark one year and 17 days; five months floating, and seven months on the mountain. They floated about 500 miles from their point of beginning to where the ark came to rest on top of Mt. Ararat in Armenia, now Turkey (elevation 17,500 feet).

8. THE NOAHIC COVENANT
(Genesis 8-9)

In chapter 6:18, we read, *"But with thee will I establish my covenant; and thou shalt come into the ark, thou, and thy sons, and thy wife, and thy sons' wives with thee."* That was the promise God made to Noah before he entered the ark. In preparing for judgment, the Lord would not destroy the righteous with the wicked. Noah believed God and his entire household was saved from the floodtide judgment. In chapter 8:1, we read, *"And God remembered Noah, and every living thing, and all the cattle that was with him in the ark: and God made a wind to pass over the earth, and the waters subsided."*

Noah opened the window of the ark and sent forth a raven; this bird of prey went to and fro until the waters had completely dried up. Noah also sent forth the little dove, but finding no rest for the sole of her foot, she returned to him, and he reached out and drew the little bird back into the ark. In seven days he sent the dove again from the ark; this time she returned with an olive leaf in her mouth. This was a miraculous sign from God that the waters were abated from off the earth. In another seven days Noah sent forth the dove for the third time. This time she did not return.

The flood was indeed a sign to man that God is holy and just and pure, and that He will deal with sin in righteousness. It served as an object lesson to us that God brings retribution for sin. This is also a type of the deluge of flame that will one day sweep our sinful world. In Matthew 24:37-39, we read,

"But as the days of Noe were, so shall also the coming of the Son of man be. For as in the days that were before the flood they were eating and drinking, marrying and giving in marriage, until the day that Noe entered into the ark, And knew not until the flood came, and took them all away; so shall also the coming of the Son of man be."

We have the principle of salvation also taught in the flood. Though the flood destroyed the earth, it saved the church. Through righteous Noah the little flock was spared. God always has his remnant in the earth through which He can work. The plagues of Egypt illustrated the same thing; they ended in death to the Egyptians, but this judgment saved the children of Israel. The cross of Calvary brings us from destruction into the bosom of the ark. Jesus Himself taught us that through death comes life.

THE RAVEN

As the destructive waves of the flood began to subside, Noah sent forth a scavenger bird which represents restlessness . The scriptures tell us he moved in and out; to and fro. This in type is the restless soul that wanders upon the face of the earth in search of peace. The raven is a filthy bird, it feeds upon earth's corruption. One writer has said this bird is a melancholy creature. He is as morbid as the food he lives upon.

THE DOVE

The foot of the little dove will not tread where the raven delights to dwell. He represents peace; he is a type of the Holy Spirit. The three outgoings of the dove are symbolic of the work of the Holy Spirit in the hearts of men. In ages before the coming of the Lord Jesus Christ, He searched the earth for a place to rest, but failing to find one, He touched the hearts of certain patriarchs here and there as God directed. This would represent the first sending forth of the dove. The second time He was sent forth, he did find a tender young branch. He plucked an olive leaf of peace and brought it to Noah. In Matthew 4:16-17, we read, *"And Jesus, when he was baptized, went up straightway out of the water: and, lo, the heavens were opened unto him, and he saw the Spirit of God descending like a dove, and lighting upon him: And lo a voice from heaven, saying, This is my beloved Son in whom I am well pleased."* Yet the third time the little dove was sent forth, he did not return to the ark; he found rest in the hearts of believers on the day of Pentecost.

THIRD DISPENSATION:
HUMAN GOVERNMENT
THIRD COVENANT: NOAHIC

As soon as Noah was told to come forth from the ark, he built an altar where he could offer sacrifices unto the Lord; no doubt under the divine direction and teaching of the Holy Spirit of God.

When the Lord smelled the sweet savour of Noah's worship, he made a promise that He would never again curse the ground for man's sake.

Verse 22: While the earth remaineth, seedtime and harvest, and cold and heat, and summer and winter, and day and night shall not cease.

In chapter 9:1, God blessed Noah and his sons, and gave them the command to multiply and fill the earth. The animals had been placed within the power of Noah and his family, and God for the first time authorized the eating of animals for food. It is possible this had been done before the flood, but without command. *"But flesh with the life thereof, which is the blood thereof, shall ye not eat" (Genesis 9:4).* God commanded them never to eat animals unless their life-blood had been drained off. The expressions of the new covenant actually begin in chapter 8:22, though the word itself is not used at that time. In these first seven verses of chapter 9, we read of some requirements of the covenant. Man is not to eat blood; man is not to kill himself or his fellowman for to murder brings the penalty of death; for man is made in the image of God.

TOKEN OF THE COVENANT

Verse 9: And I, behold, I establish my covenant with you, and with your seed after you;

Verse 10: And with every living creature that is with you, of the fowl, of the cattle, and of every beast of the earth with you; from all that go out of the ark, to every beast of the earth.

Verse 11: And I will establish my covenant with you; neither shall all flesh be cut off any more by the waters of a flood; neither shall there any more be a flood to destroy the earth.

Verse 12: And God said, This is my token of the covenant which I make between me and you and every living creature that is with you, for perpetual generations:

Verse 13: I do set my bow in the cloud, and it shall be for a token of a covenant between me and the earth.

Verse 14: And it shall come to pass, when I bring a cloud over the earth, that the bow shall be seen in the cloud:

Verse 15: And I will remember my covenant, which is between me and you and every living creature of all flesh; and the waters shall no more become a flood to destroy all flesh.

Verse 16: And the bow shall be in the cloud; and I will look upon it, that I may remember the everlasting covenant between God and every living creature of all flesh that is upon the earth.

Verse 17: And God said unto Noah, This is the token of the covenant, which I have established between me and all flesh that is upon the earth.

God blessed Noah, then established His unending covenant with him, and gave him a token of that covenant. The varied hues of the rainbow remind us of the manifold grace of God. God said that when He Himself looked, He would remember.

HAM

The end of this chapter lays bare the facts of the depravity of the Adamic nature. From the three sons of Noah, Ham, Shem and Japheth, came all the nations of the earth. Noah became a farmer and planted a vineyard, and he made wine. He lay drunk in his tent one day and Ham (father of Canaan) went inside and mocked his father's nakedness. Most scholars have recorded that the Hebrew word here for "uncovered" indicated clearly and without a doubt a deliberate act; not a mere unconscious effect of drunkenness. The word "knew" in other places in the Word speaks of the act of sex. When Noah awoke from his wine, he knew what his younger son had done unto him. And he cursed Ham's son, Canaan.

The sin of Adam resulted in his nakedness, which God Himself covered. In the Bible the nature and character of our heroes are faithfully portrayed right down to the quick. If this Word had been written without Divine Inspiration, human flaws would have been covered. But the Holy Ghost opens the putrefying sores of mankind without a Saviour. Yet, when these same stories are carried through Calvary, their shortcomings are never mentioned. Have we not learned from the fall of Adam and Noah that man at his best state is altogether vanity?

Noah's tragic fall occasioned the prophecy which came forth. His prophecy (prediction) was inspired by the Spirit of God, and gave to us an outline sketch of future nations.

Verse 25: And he said, Cused be Canaan; a servant of servants shall he be unto his brethren.

Verse 26: And he said, Blessed be the Lord God of Shem; and Canaan shall be his servant.

Verse 27: God shall enlarge Japheth, and he shall dwell in the tents of Shem; and Canaan shall be his servant.

Ham sinned as a son and was punished through his own son, Canaan. However, one must realize that this curse was not confined just to Canaan, but embraced all the descendants of Ham.

Noah also sent forth a dove (Genesis 8:8).

9. NOAH'S DESCENDANTS
(Genesis 10-11)

The existence of distinctive races and nations and languages obviously have their true origin in the book of Genesis: the book of beginnings. In the world today there are over 3,000 different tribal languages and dialects stemming from a common ancestor. Special mention is given to Nimrod who was the founder of the city of Babel or Babylon. Babylon is a name which occupies a very prominent place in the history of Jews. From the 10th chapter of Genesis, to the 17th chapter of Revelation, Babylon appears again and again; first as a powerful city, then a harlot system finally to be destroyed.

Unto the sons of Noah, Shem, Ham, and Japheth were born sons after the flood. The sons of Japheth are: Gomer, Magog, Madai, and Javan, Tubal, Mescheh, and Tiras. (These became known as the Indo-European races). Gomer became the Cimmerians on the Caspian Sea, within the boundaries of Russia. Magog (Scythians), became Russia itself. Madai became the Medes, Javan became the Greeks, or the Ionians, as they were once known.

The sons of Gomer were Ashkenaz, and Riphath, and Togarmah. The sons of Javan were Elishah, and Tarshish, Kittim, and Dodanim. Ham begat Cush and Cush begat Nimrod who became a mighty one in the earth and founder of Babel.

Cush is the same in the Bible as Ethiopia. The Cushites apparently settled on into Arabia, then crossed the Red Sea into what is known as Ethiopia. Although Cush (black) and his sons moved towards

53

Arabia and Africa, Nimrod settled in the Tigris-Euphrates valley. Cush was Ham's eldest son, and his resentment against God because of the family curse must have deepened through the years, for he named his youngest son, Nimrod, (let us rebel). Thus, Nimrod began to struggle for the ascendancy among men. One writer stated that hidden under the poor English translation, beginning with Ham, is a horrible story of desperate rebellion against God.

THE TOWER OF BABEL

The people did not want to be scattered all over the face of the earth, and they said, *"Go, let us build us a city and a tower, whose top may reach unto heaven; and let us make us a name, lest we be scattered abroad upon the face of the whole earth" (Genesis 11:4).*

It is believed that in the 11th chapter of Genesis we have a story that almost equals the importance of the great flood. The flood was universal in its effect, and so was the confusion of tongues as far as man was concerned. In Genesis 11, God divided their tongues as an expression of judgment; in Acts 2, He gave divers tongues on the day of Pentecost as an expression of grace and universal unity.

As the population grew, and Nimrod became more powerful, the people decided they should build a great city with a tower reaching into heaven. The word Babel (ba-bel) means "gate of God." In Hebrew the word "babel" means to "confuse" but these two words are not the same. Though scholars do agree that it could be a play on words, due to what happened when God came down and confounded their language. All pagan worship can be traced back to this beginning. We must note that the development of idolatry and Satan-worship was accompanied by an attempt to unify all mankind under one government. We are not told just how long the Lord watched as Nimrod constructed his tower; but we know that God's mercy extended over a period of time before He confounded the language, and scattered them all over the earth. Man has forever and eternally tried to devise a new scheme whereby he can bring God down to his own level. In Psalm 2:2 we read, *"The kings of the earth set themselves, and the rulers take counsel together, against the Lord, and against his anointed ..."* In verse 4 it says, *"He that sitteth in the heavens shall laugh: the Lord shall have them in derision."*

That great city of Babylon was built by Nimrod some two thousand years before the birth of Jesus Christ. Nimrod was a forerunner of the Man of Sin. Likely the spirit that dominated and possessed him, will also occupy the Anti-Christ. Let us also note that the great city of Nineveh, founded by Asshur, a son of Shem, became the capital of Assyria.

When the city of Babylon became the prize possession of Nebuchadnezzar, that powerful monarch, who had taken the children of Israel into captivity, he used forced labor and built an empire never equalled. According to a Bible Encyclopedia, the city was square, 14 miles on each side, making a circuit of almost 56 miles around the base of the wall which encircled it. The wall around Babylon was built of brick. According to Herodotus it was 87 feet thick and 311 feet high. Outside the great wall was a gigantic moat which surrounded the city and was kept filled with water from the Euphrates river. Drawbridges crossed the moat in front of each gate. Just inside this majestic wall was another wall not much inferior but a bit narrower, extending around the city. Thus Babylon of that day, was encompassed by two massive walls. Also, Nebuchadnezzar built hanging gardens for his wife which became one of the seven wonders of the world. The cost was untold millions.

For nearly two centuries after God scattered the people, almost nothing else is revealed about the further history of mankind. The tribes were migrating and the cultures were developing; God was the last thing on their minds. Yet one might be assured that the "Promised Seed" would come. Since man had rebelled against God, He no longer worked directly with and through the individual; in verse 10 we read the geneology (generations) of Shem, bringing us to Terah, who was the father of Abram.

Tower of Babel
"Go to, let us build . . ." (Genesis 11:4).

PART 2
THE AGE OF THE PATRIARCHS
10. THE BEGINNING OF A NATION
(Genesis 12) ABRAHAM (1898 B.C.)
FOURTH DISPENSATION: PROMISE
FOURTH COVENANT: ABRAHAMIC

THE CALL

The book of Genesis deals primarily with the history of seven men: Abel, Enoch, Noah, Abraham, Isaac, Jacob and Joseph. In each we have a distinct character of truth, and we found in each man a definite pattern of faith and a foreshadow of Christ. The call of Abram issues in the fourth dispensation, and the fourth covenant. This dispensation extended from the call of Abram to the giving of the law at Sinai. God made an unconditional promise of blessings through Abram's seed: TO THE NATION ISRAEL TO INHERIT A SPECIFIC TERRITORY FOREVER; TO THE CHURCH AS IN CHRIST; and, TO THE GENTILE NATIONS. There was a promise of blessing on all individuals and nations who bless Abram's descendants, and a curse placed on anyone who persecuted the Jews. The promise that God made to Abram and his descendants did not terminate at Sinai. Having dealt in judgment at Babel, God now deals in grace through Abraham. God would have a people all His own by the "calling of grace." It would be election by grace and not some good thing that man could offer up to God. Thus far, man had utterly failed under each dispensation.

"Hearken to me, ye that follow after righteousness, ye that seek the Lord: look unto the rock

whence ye are hewn, and to the hole of the pit whence ye are digged."

"Look to Abraham your father, and unto Sarah that bare you: for I called him alone, and blessed him and increased him" (Isaiah 51:1-2).

More than 2000 years have passed since Adam disobeyed God, and fell from his state of innocence in the garden of Eden. Repeated judgments had been visited upon mankind as a penalty for their sins and as a disciplinary measure to bring them back to their Creator.

God's call of Abram was a call from idolatry in a highly civilized nation to one of faith and obedience in a strange land.

Verse 1-3: Now the Lord had said unto Abram, Get thee out of thy country, and from thy kindred, and from thy father's house, unto a land that I will shew thee: and I will make of thee a great nation, and I will bless thee, and make thy name great; and thou shalt be a blessing: and I will bless them that bless thee, and curse him that curseth thee; and in thee shall all families of the earth be blessed.

"The God of glory appeared unto our father Abraham, when he was in Mesopotamia, before he dwelt in Charran; and said unto him, Get thee out of thy country, and from thy kindred, and come into the land which I shall show thee"

(Acts 7:2-3).

From the scriptures in Acts we note that God came to Abram in a special divine revelation, and

He gave him a call which was accompanied by promise. If Abram had refused to go, and many do, then the promise would have been given to someone else. Abram was a man of means in his home town, and he occupied a place of high position. Archaeologists have discovered that the region of Mesopotamia, from which he emigrated, had at that time reached a very high degree of culture and wealth. Ur, his city, was one of the two chief centers of Chaldean civilization. However, his ancestors and family were idolators, as we learn from Joshua 24:2: *"Your fathers dwelt on the other side of the flood in old time . . . and they served other gods. And I took your father Abraham from the other side of the flood, and led him throughout all the land of Canaan, and multiplied his seed . . ."*

Nahor begat Terah, and Terah begat Abram, Nahor, and Haran. Haran begat Lot, then he died. Nahor married Milcah, the daughter of Haran; Abram married Sarai, his half sister. Such close marriages were later forbidden in the Mosaic law; but, at this early date such marriages were not particularly dangerous from a genetic point of view and it was common practice. When we read in the scriptures, *"But Sarai was barren; she had no child" (chapter 11:30),* God is simply telling us that the child of promise must be born in the land of promise.

Abram was seventy-five years old when he answered God's call to service. We have stated Genesis is the book of Beginnings. The first eleven chapters of Genesis are really the foundation on which rests the remainder of the Bible. We could say without reservation that Abram is the most illustrious personage in ancient history.

Commands given to Abraham that followed the call:

SEPARATION

This Divine call involved obedience and separation from all Abram held near and dear. It is no small matter for one who has the call of God upon his life to break away from those he has loved and held in high esteem for so many years and start over in another place. This was exactly what God told Abram to do. He was to separate himself from all he had once cherished. Each step he took would require an altar upon which he was to sacrifice some part of the self-life. However, we view the wisdom of God in this separation. In these new surroundings, Abram would have to depend entirely upon God for guidance. Abram was from the first to the last a separated man.

As the scriptures record, Abram first answered the call upon his life with a mingled and partial obedience. God gave him three commands; he obeyed the first one, and failed in the last two. The first thing God told him to do was to leave his own country. He did that. But he did not go alone. He did not totally separate himself. Terah his father and Lot, his nephew accompanied him. Terah means "delay" and thus it happened. Terah's accompanying Abram caused a delay of five years in Haran, which means "parched." We see that Abram's response to the call of God was partial and slow, yet in the end, he obeyed. However, when we read of Abram in the New Testament, no mention is made of his failure: *"By faith Abram, when he was called to go out into a place which he should after receive for an inheritance, obeyed, and he went out, not knowing whither he went" (Hebrews 11:8).* His sins, though numerous, had been blotted out.

In Acts 7:4-5 we are told that Abram merely passed through the promised land: *"Then came he out of the land of the Chaldaeans, and dwelt in Charran: and from thence, when his father was dead, he removed him into this land, wherein ye now dwell. And he gave him none inheritance in it, no, not so much as to set his foot on: yet he promised that he would give it to him for a possession, and to his seed after him, when as yet he had no child."*

Traveling through Canaan, they arrived at a place near Shechem, and there they set up camp beside the oak at Moreh. (Shecham signifies shoulder, the place of strength; oak of Moreh, means instruction.)

Strength is found when we are totally obedient to God, and when we follow the path He has designed for our lives. It is then that we learn of His wisdom and knowledge, and taste the joy of true fellowship with our Creator.

Verse 7: And the Lord appeared unto Abram, and said, Unto thy seed will I give this land: and There builded he an altar unto the Lord, who appeared unto him.

This appearance to Abram was the Lord Jesus Christ, since we are told in the Word that no man has at any time seen God. *"No man hath seen God at any time; the only begotten Son, which is in the bosom of the Father, he hath declared him" (John 1:18).* We can further establish this truth by reading Exodus 33:20: *"And he said, Thou canst not see my face: for there shall no man see me and live."*

FAMINE IN THE LAND

Abram moved on southward to the hill country between Bethel on the west and Ai on the east, and there he camped and made another altar where he prayed. He moved on southward to the Negev, stopping some along the way. (Bethel means "house of God," while Ai means "a heap of ruin.") It is interesting to note that Abram continued to journey southward, which would lead him right on into Egypt. When famine hit the land of Canaan, his face was already set for Egypt. Now we encounter the second failure of Abram.

Verse 10: And there was a famine in the land: and Abram went down into Egypt to sojourn there; for the famine was grievous in the land.

Things weren't adding up for this man of faith. He had left his homeland to follow the Lord, and found the land flowing with milk and honey not only filled with the Canaanites, but there was a grievous famine in the land. Egypt is a type of the world, and it symbolizes the arm of flesh. In Isaiah 31:3, we read, *"Woe to them that go down to Egypt for help and stay on horses, and trust in chariots, because they are many; and in horsemen, because they are very strong; but they look not unto the Holy One of Israel, neither seek the Lord:"*

Abram's faith was sorely tried. He would be required to believe God in spite of famine in the land of promise. Down in Egypt Abram practiced deception and denied that Sarai was his wife, thus endangering her honor, and their very lives. Yet God remained faithful. In 2 Timothy 2:13, we read, *"If we believe not yet He abideth faithful: He cannot deny Himself."*

When Abram was close to the border of Egypt, he asked Sarai, his wife, to tell everyone that she was his sister for she was very beautiful, and he reasoned that when the Egyptians saw her they would kill him and take her.

It happened just that way. The palace aids praised Sarai to the king, and she was taken into his harem. Abram was given many gifts because of her; but the Lord sent a terrible plague upon Pharaoh's household, and the king demanded to know what was going on. He asked Abram why he was willing to let him marry Sarai, claiming her to be his sister. Abram had to admit to the king that he and Sarai had agreed to lie lest the king kill him and take her as his wife.

Pharaoh had been convinced by the plagues that God was with Abram. He sent them out of the land, rich in cattle, silver and gold. So Sarai, Abram and Lot left Egypt and traveled south until he reached Bethel, the place where his tent had been before they entered Egypt because of famine.

11. THE COVENANT RENEWED
(Genesis 15-17)

We will briefly mention here that both Abram and his nephew, Lot, had so greatly increased in goods that they had to come to a parting of the ways. In chapter 13:2, we read, *"And Abram was very rich in cattle, in silver, and in gold."* It is of special interest for us to note that the Holy Ghost pointed out the abundance of Abram's riches by the use of the word "very." In the New Testament, Jesus said that we were to have life, and have it in abundance. In other words, we are to have the same call, dedication, and prosperity as Abram. *"The thief cometh not, but for to steal, and to kill, and to destroy: I am come that they might have life, and that they might have it more abundantly"* *(John 10:10).*

After his disobedience in Egypt, Abram returned to the house of God for a time of repentance and refreshing. God had divinely intervened down in Egypt, because Sarai was chosen to bring forth the promised heir. Lot, too, was very wealthy and the land cound not support both of them. When strife entered in between their two herdsmen, Abram gave Lot his choice of any of the land upon which to settle.

Lot lifted up his eyes and beheld the well-watered plains of Jordan, before God destroyed it, and decided that was what he wanted. Lot journeyed east, and they separated themselves from each other. Abram dwelt in the land of Canaan; Lot moved his tent as far as Sodom where the men were wicked beyond the imagination. Lot is a type of the flesh; Abram is a type of the spirit. Both cannot dwell together in unity. This is another phase of the separation for Abram demanded by God. In 13:14-18, we read where the land is given unto Abram, and natural posterity is promised: *"And the Lord said unto Abram, after that Lot was separated from him, Lift up now thine eyes, and look from the place where thou art northward, and southward, and eastward, and westward: For all the land which thou seest, to thee will I give it, and to thy seed for ever. And I will make thy seed as the dust of the earth: so that if a man can number the dust of the earth, then shall thy seed also be numbered. Arise, walk through the land in the length of it and in the breadth of it; for I will give it unto thee. Then Abram removed his tent, and came and dwelt in the plain of Mamre, which is in Hebron and built there an altar unto the Lord."* Note that God did not speak to Abram of His promises until he had separated him from Lot.

ABRAM DELIVERS LOT

Lot had made his home in a city that was built by man, but was destroyed by the Lord. In Genesis 14, we have the record of the years of war that had been going on between the kings of the land: Amraphel, king of Shinar; Aroch, King of Ellasar; Ched-or-laomer, king of Elam; and Tidal, king of Goiim — fought against: Bera, king of Sodom; Birsha, king of Gomorrah; Shinab, king of Admach; Shemeber, king of Zeboiim; and the king of Bela (Zoar), as it was called later. The kings of Sodom and Gomorrah joined together in the Siddim Valley (the valley of the Salt Sea), to fight for their freedom from Ched-or-laomer, having been subject to him for twelve long years. As it happened, this valley was full of slim pits. When the armies of the kings of Sodom and Gomorrah fled, some slipped into the pits, and the remainder fled towards the mountains. When the victors plundered Sodom and Gomorrah to gather the spoils of battle, they took Lot with them. When Abram learned of Lot's plight, he gathered his household of men together to rescue his nephew. His army consisted of 318 men; but he was going in the will of the Lord. He divided his men into several groups and attached the enemy in the dark from different directions. It was the Lord that delivered the enemy into his hands, and Abram restored Lot all his goods, and his household.

GOD REVEALS HIMSELF AS EL ELYON

Verse 18: And Melchizedek, king of Salem, brought forth bread and wine; and he was the priest of the most high God (El Elyon).

Verse 19: And he blessed him, and said, Blessed be Abram of the most high God, possessor of heaven and earth:

When the battle was over, the kings went out to meet Abram as he returned from the slaughter of Ched-or-laomer, and Melchizedek, king of Salem (Peace), brought forth the bread and the wine to refresh Abram. He blessed Abram, and Abram gave him one-tenth of all that he possessed. This is the first tithe offering. In Hebrews 7:2, we read, *"To whom also Abraham gave a tenth part of all; first being by interpretation King of righteousness, and after that also King of Salem, which is, King of peace;"* Jesus was appointed after the order of Melchizedek rather than after the order and rank of Aaron, the high priest. When there is a change in the priesthood, there is, of necessity an alteration of the law concerning the priesthood. Our Lord came from the tribe of Judah, no member of which had ministered at the altar. Moses mentioned nothing about priests in connection with that tribe. Jesus was set forth by the taking of an oath for we read in Hebrews 7:16-17, *"Who is made, not after the law of a carnal commandment, but after the power of an endless life. For he testifieth, Thou art a priest forever after the order of Melchisedek."* We should also note that this is the first mention of the city of Jerusalem.

The king of Sodom wanted Abram to take the goods and give the persons to him, and Abram replied that he had solemnly promised the Lord that he would not take a thing from the king, not even a shoe lace, lest the king should brag that he was the one who had helped to make Abram rich. Abram would have no part of the flesh!

ADONAI

In chapter 15, the covenant is confirmed, and a spiritual seed is promised to Abram. Abram had a vision, and the Lord (Adonai) talked with him. It is interesting to observe four striking phrases that are used for the first time here in chapter 15, but each will be repeated throughout the Word of God in many variations. (1) the Word of the Lord came, (2) the Lord God is a shield, (3) fear not, (4) believed. In Romans 4:20, we read, *"He staggered not at the promise of God through unbelief; but was strong in faith, giving glory to God."*

The Word of the Lord came to Abram concerning two great matters. He spoke with him about "fear"

69

and about the promised heir. More than ten years had passed since he entered Canaan, and there must have been times when Abram wondered about the promises God had made since nothing had really happened to encourage him in the faith. Three successive promises had rekindled his hopes, but they seemed as far from realization as ever. Not a sign of a child, and the years were closing in on Abram and his wife, Sarai. It was under these circumstances that the Word of the Lord spoke to him words of encouragement and enlightment as to the promises.

Verse 1: After these things the word of the Lord came unto Abram in a vision, saying, Fear not, Abram: I am thy shield, and they exceeding great reward.

Verse 2: And Abram said, Lord God, what wilt thou give me, seeing I go childless, and the steward of my house is this Eliezer of Damascus?

Verse 3: And Abram said, Behold, to me thou hast given no seed; and, lo, one born in my house is mine heir.

Verse 4: And, behold, the word of the Lord came unto him, saying, This shall not be thine heir, but he that shall come forth out of thine own bowels shall be thine heir.

Verse 5: And he brought him forth abroad, and said, Look now toward heaven, and tell the stars, if thou be able to number them: and he said unto him, So shall thy seed be.

Verse 6: And he believed in the Lord; and he counted it to him for righteousness.

Fear is the opposite of faith; God spoke to Abram and said for him to enter into full-faith, dismissing all fears that the promises would not be fulfilled. When a heart is full of faith, there is no room for the anxieties and fears of this life. Abram would have to believe God when, in fact, he and his wife had gone past the age of child-bearing. He had to believe God for the land flowing with milk and honey while his enemies possessed the land. In Romans 8:25, we are told, *"If we hope for that we see not, then do we with patience wait for it."* Abram learned well his lessons in endurance even when God was silent. He asked God for a sign or a token that would serve as an eternal encouragement.

Verse 9: And he said unto him, Take me an heifer of three years old, and a she-goat of three years old, and a ram of three years old, and a turtledove, and a young pigeon.

Verse 10: And he took unto him all these, and divided them in the midst, and laid each piece one against another: but the birds divided he not.

Verse 11: And when the fowls came down upon the carcases, Abram drove them away.

Take Me a heifer . . . Christ in type before us here. This was to be his sign. It has been pointed out by another that each of the three animals named were tamed ones. They were willing servants of man's need. Each one foreshadowed a distinctive aspect of Christ's perfection and work. The heifer of three years seemed to have pointed to the freshness of His vigor; the goat gave the sin-offering aspect; and the ram was the animal that, in the Levitical offerings, was connected specially with consecration. The birds told of One from heaven; the three years mentioned three times, probably suggestive of the time of our Lord's sacrifice, offered after three years of service. We must note that death passed over all, for without the shedding of blood there is no remission —no remission means no inheritance. The dividing of the animals indicated that this sacrifice was to form the basis for a covenant. The fowls in type are the demonic forces ready to devour the sacrifices placed on the altars of life. It was Abram, not God, who stood firm against the devourers. Through the Lord Jesus, we have the authority to stand firm against the wiles of the devil. The birds of prey have attempted to keep Israel from her true inheritance: the land which God Himself promised to her. Egypt sought to detain them; then they faced the birds of Babylon, Greece, Rome, and today, the Arabs.

Verse 12: And when the sun was going down, a deep sleep fell upon Abram; and lo, an horror of great darkness fell upon him.

ISRAEL'S CAPTIVITY PREDICTED

God put Abram into a deep sleep just as he had Adam when he opened his rib to bring forth his wife, Eve. The sun went down and a great darkness fell upon him. God spoke to him of a nation not yet developed, and of a deliverance not yet needed.

Verse 13: And he said unto Abram, Know for a surety that thy seed shall be a stranger in a land that is not theirs, and shall serve them; and they shall afflict them four hundred years;

Verse 14: And also that nation, whom they shall serve, will I judge: and afterward shall they come out with great substance.

Verse 15: And thou shalt go to thy fathers in peace; thou shalt be buried in a good old age.

It was a long and dark prospect which unfolded itself before Abram while he slept in the bosom of the Father. God told Abram that in the fourth generation, his descendants would return from captivity to their land, for the wicked nations living in Canaan would not be ready for punishment until then.

Verse 17: And it came to pass, that, when the sun went down, and it was dark, behold a smoking furnace, and a burning lamp that passed between those pieces.

Verse 18: And in the same day the Lord made a covenant with Abram, saying, unto thy seed have I given this land, from the river of Egypt unto the great river, the river Euphrates.

The smoking furnace was a symbol of the presence of God. The furnace was a small pot with which the silversmiths and goldsmiths melted down their precious ores so that the dross could be drawn off, leaving the refined and pure elements. The Word of God tells us that the trial of our faith is much more precious than gold which perishes, though it be tried in the fire (I Peter 1:7). The children of Israel would go through the fiery furnace of affliction before they would see the promises fulfilled. The smoking furnace and the burning lamp, as the symbol of the presence of God, taught Abram of the Divine Presence of God during all their afflictions. Much more is suggested which we must bypass for lack of space. The passing between the parts is also to be noted. The dividing of the bodies of the animals offered for sacrifice was a most solemn method of taking an oath according to both Greek and Hebrew authorities. The parties to the oath walked around the two heaps of flesh in the path of a figure eight. God judged the men who broke the covenant. When Abram divided the bodies of the animals, he was preparing the place for the God of Glory to walk.

In chapter 16, we find unbelief casting its dark shadow across the spirit of Abram. He decided to help God. What greater contrast could we find between the happenings in chapter 15, and what is presented in this 16th chapter of Genesis. In chapter 15, we view Abram as the man of faith; he is seen walking in the Spirit of God, holding counsel with the Most Holy Lord. Here he falls back to relying upon his own flesh, and hearkening to Sarai, his wife.

HAGAR, TYPE OF FLESH

Sarai took her Egyptian maid, and gave her to Abram for his second wife because as yet there had been no child born into the home. Where was the child of promise? Had God forgotten His covenant? Sarai was not acting out of line with the custom of her day, but she was out of line and out of step with the covenant that God had made with her husband, Abram. But when Hagar, the maid, realized that she was pregnant, she despised her mistress, and became very haughty and proud of herself. Abram gave Sarai permission to punish Hagar for her attitude, so Sarai beat her, and Hagar fled into the wilderness where the angel of the Lord found her and sent her back to her mistress. He said, "Return and submit, and I will greatly multiply your seed. He told her she was with child, and that the child would be a boy. She was told to name the boy Ishmael (God hears) because God has heard your woes. Ishmael would always be wild; he would be against everyone, and have many enemies.

Ishmael lapsed into unbelief, and became the progenitor of the Arabs, and the enemy of the Jewish people. Mohammed, founder of Islam, came from a seed line of Ishmael. Islam is the world religion even today, and is perhaps the closest to Christianity; thus, it is most difficult to penetrate it with the Gospel of Jesus Christ as Saviour. Abram was now 86 years old when his son, Ishmael, was born unto him.

EL SHADDAI, ALMIGHTY GOD

In chapter 17:1-3, when Abram was 99 years old, Almighty God appeared to him, and reviewed their covenant. It had been thirteen long years since the birth of Ishmael, and still no heir in his home. God appeared and gave Abram a Divine summons: walk before Me, and be thou perfect. God told him that He would prepare the contract between the two of them, and that Abram would be the father of many nations. Abram was so overwhelmed he fell on his face and in that worshipful attitude, God talked with him. In all this we have the remedy for Abram's many failures. God never demands anything that He Himself has not already provided.

Verse 5: Neither shall thy name any more be called Abram, but thy name shall be Abraham; for a father of many nations have I make thee.

His name was being changed from Abram (exalted father) to Abraham (father of many nations). In Hebrew, God added one letter to

Abram's name, the letter is formed by breathing. The Lord took an "h" out of His unprounounceable name, YHWH, and put it in the name of Abram. *"From this point on you are a part of ME."*

God breathed the breath of life into the lifeless clay and man became Adam; His breath upon the nature of Abram brought forth fruitfulness to a man 99 years old, and to Sarai who was past the age of child bearing. One might be likely to ask why God waited so long to fulfill his promise to Abram for a son which He had promised to him years prior to his birth. We have part of the answer as we read I Corinthians 1:29, *"That no flesh should glory in his presence."* Man must come to the end of himself lest he consider in his heart that he has helped God. God is a supernatural God, and His works are supernatural.

Here we must comment on the "I will's" in chapter 17. *"I will make my covenant . . . I will multiply thee . . . I will make thee exceeding fruitful . . . I will make nations of thee . . . I will establish my covenant between me and thee and thy seed after thee . . . I will be a God to thee and thy seed after thee . . . I will give unto thee and unto thy seed the land . . . I will be their God"*

Grace calls for faithfulness; an obligation goes with such a high calling. When we learn that there is no power within us to fulfill our side of the covenant, we will trust God that He does not break covenant because of our unfaithfulness. God chose that circumcision would be a token of the covenant. In verse 10 it is used for the first time. Circum (Latin) means "around" like our word circumference. The other half of the word is "to cut."

God said there was to be a mark upon the bodies of all His people, as a sign that He had cut the covenant with them, and they were to cut away all the hindering weights that would keep them from serving Him. God wants His people to be sealed unto Himself by the shedding of blood." Eight is "new order" just as there were eight people who entered the ark of new beginnings. It is on the eight day that all male children would be circumcised to mark the beginning of the covenant God made with their fathers.

SARAI'S NAME CHANGED

Verse 15: And God said unto Abraham, As for Sarai thy wife, thou shalt not call her name Sarai, but Sarah shall her name be.

Sarah means "princess with God." She was to become the mother of many nations. She would have a son and they were to call him Isaac (laughter), *"I will establish my covenant with him for an everlasting covenant, and with his seed after him . . . I have blessed Ishmael . . . I will make of him a great nation . . . But my covenant will I establish with Isaac . . ." (Verses 19, 20, 21).*

Note that when God changed Abram to Abraham, the letters "ha" were added. Also, with Sarai, we note "ah" a "breathie" sound was involved. God breathed new life upon old clay.

12. INTERCESSION
(Genesis 18-19)

Abraham was now to be totally separated from his nephew, Lot. Abraham is the father of the faithful; Lot is a type of the flesh or worldly Christian. Abraham walked by faith; Lot walked by sight. By the oak grove in Mamre (fatness), God appeared once again unto Abraham on a hot summer afternoon. When Abraham saw three men coming in his direction, he jumped up and ran to welcome them. He insisted that the travelers stop and rest under the shade of the old tree while he got water to refresh them by washing their feet. Such words as ran, bowed, wash, rest, fetch, hastened, quickly, and dressed, give a beautiful picture of eastern hospitality. Abraham ran after them, he bowed before them; he insisted he be allowed to wash their feet, and feed them before they continued in the heat of the day. While they were eating under the tree, they said unto him, *"Where is Sarah thy wife?"*

Verse 10: And he said, I will certainly return unto thee according to the time of life; and, lo, Sarah thy wife shall have a son. And Sarah heard it in the tent door, which was behind him.

The Lord was sitting with his back to Sarah when he told Abraham that his wife would have a son. Sarah laughed within herself and He asked Abraham why Sarah had laughed. This was to be a supernatural birth. *"Is anything to hard for the Lord . . .?"* This was the pre-incarnate Christ talking over life's situations with Abraham, A FRIEND OF GOD. We must contrast this story with the announcement of the birth of our Lord in

Luke 1:37: *"For with God nothing shall be impossible."* To which young Mary replied, *"... be it unto me according to thy word ..." (verse 38).* (Sarah was heard only by the Lord at that time; He knows and hears all things.)

The men rose up and looked toward Sodom, and Abraham walked along with them and they talked further. The Lord said, *"Shall I hide from Abraham that thing which I do; Seeing that Abraham shall surely become a great and mighty nation, and all the nations of the earth shall be blessed in him" (verse 17-18)?* What amazing grace and favor!

As the men turned to go in toward Sodom to check out the wicked city, Abraham began to plead with the Lord who lingered for a while to discuss the situation with him. After all, Lot was living within the city gates, implying he was an important man in Sodom.

Verse 23: And Abraham drew near, and said, Wilt thou also destroy the righteous with the wicked?

Verse 24: Peradventure there be fifty righteous within the city: wilt thou also destroy and not spare the place for the fifty righteous that are therein?

Verse 25: ... shalt not the Judge of all the earth do right?

To this plea the Lord agreed. If He could find 50 righteous men in the city, He would not destroy it. Abraham humbled himself before the Lord to be able to speak yet another time in behalf of the people. The Lord said He would not destroy the city if 45 righteous men could be found. Abraham questioned the Lord again, and the Lord agreed that if he could locate even 40 righteous men in the city, He would spare the entire population. How about 30 ... only 20 ... maybe 10? To each of those pleadings the Lord agreed to spare the city.

In chapter 19, we are told that when the angels reached the city, Lot was sitting in the gate, and he welcomed them warmly as they approached. (The elders always sat at the gate of the city.) He insisted on showing them the hospitality of his home for the night. He knew they were angels. They went with him, and he set a feast before them. Just as the household was preparing to retire for the night, the wicked men of the city, both young and old, demanded that Lot bring the men to them so they could rape them. Lot offered his virgin daughters in their stead. The Sodomites refused and began to break down the door. By offering his virgin daughters, Lot tried to compromise good with evil. This story reveals God's attitudes, views, and judgments against homosexuality, In Romans 1:18-32, we read it from the Word, *"For the wrath of God is revealed from heaven against all ungodliness and unrighteousness of men, who hold the truth in unrighteousness; Because that which may be known of God is manifest in them; for God hath shewed it unto them . . . so they are without excuse: Because that, when they knew God, they glorified him not as God, neither were thankful; but became vain in their imaginations, and their foolish heart was darkened. Professing themselves to be wise, they became fools, And changed the glory of the*

80

uncorruptible God into an image made like to corruptible man, and to birds, and four-footed beasts, and creeping things. Wherefore God also gave them up to uncleanness through the lust of their own hearts, to dishonour their own bodies between themselves: Who changed the truth of God into a lie, . . . God gave them up unto vile affections . . . their women did change the natural use into that which is against nature: And likewise also the men, leaving the natural use of the woman, burned in their lust one toward another; men with men, . . . God gave them over to a reprobate mind, . . . Being filled with all unrighteousness, fornication, wickedness, covetousness, maliciousness; full of envy, murder, debate, deceit, malignity; whispers, backbiters, haters of God . . . Without understanding, covenantbreakers, without natural affection . . . Who knowing the judgment of God, that they which commit such things are worthy of death, not only do the same, but have pleasure in them that do them."

The angels reached out and grabbed Lot, and pulled him into the house, and bolted the door. They warned Lot to gather his family quickly, for God was ready to rain down fire and brimstone from heaven on Sodom and Gomorrah.

Lot's first step towards backsliding was when he lifted up his eyes and beheld the well-watered plains of Jordan, (before God destroyed Sodom and Gomorrah); his second step towards backsliding was when he pitched his tent toward Sodom. His third step towards backsliding was in the fact that he became an important man in the city. Lot showed his own lack of spirituality when he tried to reason with the men, offering his own daughters in the bargain. Though he rushed out and warned his daughters fiances that God was about to destroy the city, when morning came, and the angels were urging him on, Lot hesitated to go, leaving heel marks all the way. He even pleaded that he be allowed to go into Zoar, a city nearby, rather than into the mountains. Lot's wife looked back at the destruction, though God had warned them to look straight ahead. She is a type of our looking back into the world after we have been delivered from its pitfalls. We cannot look back in retrospect, desiring and regretting. Josephus, the Jewish historian, tells that he saw pillars of salt still standing in his day. Jesus warned, *"No man, having put his hand to the plough, and looking back, is fit for the kingdom of God," (Luke 9:62).*

Just as Lot was safely delivered from the city, fire fell from heaven and destroyed all the inhabitants of Sodom and Gomorrah, never again to be inhabited.

We are told that Abraham rose early that morning, and he hurried out to the place where he had stood the day before with the Lord, looked across the plain, and saw the smoke and fumes of the cities rising higher and higher.

Fear fell upon Lot in the city of Zoar because of people, and he took his two daughters and fled to a cave. They plotted to fill him with wine, so they could lay with him, and preserve the family seed. The older daughter had a son by him, and called him Moab, and he became the ancestory of the nation of Moabites. The younger daughter had a son by her father, and named him Benammi, and he became the ancestor of the nation of the Ammonites.

13. ABRAHAM'S LAPSE AT GERAR
(Genesis 20)

Abraham moved south to the Negev, and settled between Kadesh and Shur. It was not by accident that Sarah fell into the hands of an alien king for the second time. She was a beautiful woman, and in Egypt the Pharoah took her into his harems. There is a special reason why God intervened so quickly where Abimelech was concerned.

In chapter twelve we are brought face to face with the fact that she was treated as one of Pharoah's wives, until he learned the truth. In the chapter before us, we are told that God appeared to Abimelech, King of Gerar, in a dream, and told him he was the same as a dead man if he touched Sarah. Only a few months had passed since God had spoken to Abraham about Sarah having a son. If Abimelech had taken her for his wife, there could have been question as to Isaac's real father. The royal seed line had to be protected.

Abraham displayed the true nature of all flesh even in his latter years. It is not clear just why Abraham left the place where God had visited with him to discuss Sodom and Gomorrah; but we find him again in a foreign country, lying about his own wife to save his life.

Verse 7: Now therefore restore the man his wife; for he is a prophet, and he should pray for thee, and thou shalt live: and if thou restore her not, know thou that thou shalt surely die, thou, and all that are thine.

That dream came to the king in the night time; the next verse tells us that the king lost no time getting Sarah out of his presence, and back into the hands of her husband. He rose early in the morning for he was afraid. Abimelech upbraided Abraham for what he had done. He even asked what he had done to deserve such betrayal. The king called Abraham's actions a "vile deed."

Verse 11: And Abraham said, Because I thought, Surely the fear of God is not in this place; and they will slay me for my wife's sake.

In verse 13 we are told that this agreement came between Sarah and Abraham when he left his homeland, taking her with him. He had asked her to say she was his brother wherever they wandered. Abimelech gave them sheep and oxen, and servants, and offered to allow them to live in the land wherever it pleased them to settle.

Verse 17: So Abraham prayed unto God: and God healed Abimelech, and his wife, and his maidservants; and they bare children.

Verse 18: For the Lord had fast closed up all the wombs of the house of Abimelech, because of Sarah, Abraham's wife.

Perhaps we can find a partial answer to the incredible way Abraham acted in Proverbs 27:19: *"As in water face answereth to face, so the heart of man to man."* The rest of the answer will come as we remember our own departures and lapses from the walk of faith. It is in such an hour of our lives that God's light of mercy and grace shines the brightest in our behalf. We never know what is in our heart until circumstances arise to draw it out. When Abimelech confronted Abraham for his sin, all he saw was a man who had lied and caused him to be troubled in his own spirit; but God spoke of Abraham as a prophet who would pray for the household of Abimelech. Abraham is our example that God's election stands sure. Deeply important are the lessons we can learn from the life of Abraham.

PROMISES
TO ABRAHAM:

1.	I will show you the land	12:1
2.	Make of you a great nation	12:2
3.	Bless you	12:2; 22:17
4.	Make your name great	12:2
5.	You will be a blessing	12:2
6.	I will bless them that bless you	12:3
7.	Will curse them that curse you	12:3
8.	In you all nations (families) will be blessed	12:3; 22:18
9.	I will give this land to your seed forever	12:7; 13:14-17
10.	I will make your seed as the dust in number	13:16
11.	I am your shield	15:1
12.	I am your great reward	15:1
13.	Your own son shall be your heir	15:2-4
14.	Your seed shall be as the stars in number	15:5; 22:17
15.	Your seed shall be strangers and oppressed 400 years	15:13
16.	I will punish their oppressors	15:14
17.	I will bring your seed out of bondage (fulfilled, Ex. 12:32-38, 41)	15:14-16
18.	I will bless your seed with great material substance	15:14
19.	You will die in peace	15:15
20.	You will be buried in a good old age	15:15
21.	I will make an everlasting covenant with you	17:4, 7
22.	I will multiply you exceedingly	17:2; 22:17
23.	I have made you the father of many nations	17:5, 6
24.	I will make you exceedingly fruitful	17:6
25.	Kings shall come from you	17:6
26.	I will establish an everlasting covenant with your seed	17:7
27.	I will be a God to you and your seed	17:7-8
28.	I will bless your wife	17:16
29.	I will give you a son of her	17:16-19
30.	She shall be a mother of many nations	17:16
31.	Kings shall come of her	17:16

32.	I will establish my everlasting covenant with Isaac and his seed	17:19, 21
33.	I will bless Ishmael	17:20
34.	I will make him fruitful	17:20
35.	I will multiply him exceedingly	17:20
36.	Twelve princes shall he beget	17:20
37.	I will make him a great nation	17:20
38.	Sarah shall have a son next year	17:21
39.	I will not destroy Sodom if I find fifty righteous	18:26
40.	I will not destroy Sodom for forty-five righteous	18:28
41.	I will not destroy Sodom for forty righteous	18:29
42.	I will not destroy Sodom for thirty righteous	18:30
43.	I will not destroy Sodom for twenty righteous	18:31
44.	I will not destroy Sodom for ten righteous	18:32
45.	In Isaac shall your seed be called	21:12
46.	I will multiply your seed as sand	22:17
47.	Your seed shall be victory over enemies	22:17
48.	In your seed shall all nations be blessed	22:18

14. THE BIRTH OF ISAAC
(Genesis 21)   (1845 B.C.)

At last the promised heir is born into the household of Abraham. God is a covenant-keeping God, and what He has promised, He will deliver.

Verse 1-2: And the Lord visited Sarah as he had said, and the Lord did unto Sarah as he had spoken. For Sarah conceived, and bare Abraham a son in his old age, at the set time of which God had spoken to him.

Many years had passed since God first talked with Abraham and promised him a child. How could he be the father of many nations when no son had been born into his household? God is not dependent upon the creature, but the creature is dependent upon God. Everything is definitely prepared beforehand by God. In verse 2, we read *"... at the set time"* which places the entire matter in the hands of a capable Lord. In this we have the blessed fruit of patient waiting. We are also allowed to see the spiritual side of Abraham and the carnal side. The Holy Spirit has chosen to show us both the weakness and the strength of the man who was destined to be the father of all nations.

There were those sublime moments when Abraham knew God as his portion and protector; then there were the times when he lapsed into sin that only Calvary could erase. Thus, we see ourselves in the lives of each of the Patriarchs. It was not until God's promise of Isaac was fulfilled reality that Abraham could fully understand the futility of trying to help God accomplish His eternal purpose. Ishmael was of no use whatsoever as far as

God's promise was concerned. Ishmael was born of the flesh; Isaac was the child of the Spirit and promise. Note the four-fold types found in Isaac: (1) of the Church as composed of the spiritual children of Abraham, (2) of Christ as the Son "obedient unto death," (3) of the Christ as the Bridegroom of a called-out Bride, (4) of the new nature of the believer as "born of the Spirit."

In the Hebrew we are told that Isaac is not a word but a sound. It is the sound of laughter. It would be like "ha, ha, ha." So whenever Sarah called Isaac, she would really be saying, "Ha Ha Ha, please come wash your hands!"

According to the covenant seal, Abraham circumcised his son eight days after he was born. According to Jewish custom, children are weaned anywhere from three to five years old. It is always a time for festivities. On that special day Sarah saw Ishmael, son of the bondwoman, mocking Isaac. She demanded that Abraham cast both, Hagar and Ishmael, from her presence.

Verse 10: Wherefore she said unto Abraham, Cast out this bondwoman and her son: for the son of this bondwoman shall not be heir with my son, even with Isaac.

One can readily see that the birth of Isaac brought out the true nature of Ishmael. Is it not the way of all flesh to persecute and mock those who walk in the Spirit? No communion is possible between Ishmael and Isaac. One is the son of a slave, and the other is the son of the free woman; One is the child of natural powers, the other the child of God's supernatural powers. If grace is to reign, law must be removed. In

Galatians 4:28-31, we read, *"Now we, brethren, as Isaac was, are the children of promise. But as then he that was born after the flesh persecuted him that was born after the Spirit, even so it is now. Nevertheless, what saith the scripture? Cast out the bondwoman and her son; for the son of the bondwoman shall not be heir with the son of the freewoman. So, then, brethren, we are not children of the bondwoman, but of the free."*

This thing grieved Abraham, but God had spoken to him and told him to listen to Sarah. This was not an easy matter for Abraham. Ishmael had been his son for nearly fourteen years. It is interesting to note that in the chapter we have before us, not once is the name "Ishmael" used. He is referred to as the lad, or the son of the bondwoman.

Verse 12: And God said unto Abraham, Let it not be grievous in thy sight because of the lad, and because of thy bondwoman; in all that Sarah hath said unto thee, hearken unto her voice; for in Isaac shall thy seed be called.

Verse 13: And also of the son of the bondwoman will I make a nation, because he is thy seed.

The Arabs have been blessed because they are the seed of Abraham, not because they enter into the inheritance of the promised land.

So Abraham rose early the next day to send Hagar and Ishmael from their home. He prepared food and water for the journey, and sent them away into the wilderness of Beersheba. Hagar had been wandering aimlessly around, crying aloud, when the Angel of the Lord spoke to her from heaven. He opened her eyes and she saw a well; she refilled their jugs with water, and as they refreshed there in the desert, God blessed the boy and promised to make a good nation of him. The lad grew up in the wilderness and became an expert archer.

Before we leave our story, let us point out that it was not through any merit of his own that Ishmael received blessing from God. He had no claims upon God, or Abraham. Every blessing is from above and given to us by a God of love and mercy. No man can come to the Lord on his own merits. All of us have sinned and fallen short of the glory of God. Hagar and the lad were sent into the desert, far away from the house of faith, without much more than a bottle of water and little food. Man's extremity is God's opportunity.

Hagar represents Mt. Sinai, the law, and the law had to be cast out with no provision made for the flesh. One writer has so aptly said, ". . . the law must be cast out before grace can triumph. This ancient family quarrel is recorded by God in meticulous detail to teach us that the legalists must always hate the children of grace, and that the former must be cast out by the latter." There could be no compromise. God will never allow grace to be mocked by the law. The law brings bondage. The law of grace sets us free. There are many today who resent the fact that the Jews have been singled out as God's chosen and peculiar people. God is the creator of man. Can He not do with us as He chooses? The very name "saints" and "elect" are offensive to many.

Flesh has no faith. When Hagar ran out of water, she left the lad and cried, *"Let me not see the death*

90

of the child." She was unable to reflect back to the time she ran away from Sarah, and God found her and promised that her son would be the leader of a mighty nation. Flesh has to see it. Faith believes the Word of God and waits for the manifestation of the promise. In the Amplified New Testament, II Thessalonians 3:3, we read of the faithfulness of God: *"Yet the Lord is faithful and He will strengthen (you) and set you on a firm foundation and guard you from the evil (one)."* In the Amplified New Testament, Hebrews 6:18, we read that He cannot change, and that He is bound by His own oath: *"This was so that by two unchangeable things (His promise, and His oath), in which it is impossible for God ever to prove false or deceive us, we who have fled (to Him) for refuge might have mighty indwelling strength and strong encouragement to grasp and hold fast the hope appointed for us and set before (us)."*

Ishmael married an Egyptian. Legalism always hooks up with the world. Egypt was the child of Ham, the son of Noah, who was cursed for looking upon the nakedness of his father.

Abraham lived in tents. Today they are still widely used. (On the road to Hebron)

91

15. GOD WILL PROVIDE HIMSELF
(Genesis 22)

Up to this point Abraham had learned many names of God. In chapter 14, he called upon El Elyon, The Most High God. In chapter 17:1-2, He is the El Shaddai, the God all Sufficient, Dispenser and Giver of all gifts. The God of Glory had appeared to him; he had some knowledge of Jehovah. In chapter 21:33, he built an altar and called upon El Olam, the God of successive ages. In this chapter he is taken through the greatest testing period of his entire life. He built an altar and called upon God, Jehovah-Jireh, meaning the Lord will Provide Himself a Sacrifice.

Verse 1: And it came to pass after these things, that God did tempt Abraham, and said unto him, Abraham: and he said, Behold, here I am.

Verse 2: And he said, Take now thy son, thine only son Isaac, whom thou lovest, and get thee into the land of Moriah; and offer him there for a burnt offering upon one of the mountains which I will tell thee of.

The Hebrew word for "tempt" is *"nasah"* which means "prove" or "approved." This in no way suggested that Abraham was being tempted to do evil. In James 1:13, we read that no man is tempted of God to do evil.

Verse 3: And Abraham rose up early in the morning, and saddled his ass, and took two of his young men with him, and Isaac his son, and clave the wood for the burnt offering, and rose up and went unto the place which God had told him.

The testing period of Abraham was still taking place. To ask him to sacrifice his son, or any human being, was a command that the idolatorous nations from which he had separated himself would give. At some point in his early life, Abraham had probably either witnessed such rituals, or had heard of them around the family circles. God was asking for total and complete trust. He surely must have quickly reflected upon his past, when God spoke to him with this command. But just as quickly, he rose up and made the preparation for his journey. Yes, God did put Abraham to the test of perfect obedience and submission. Abraham was facing the greatest test of his life.

Moriah means "chosen of God," or "The Lord will Provide." In verse 2 we read "*. . . get thee into the land of Moriah and offer him there for a burnt offering upon one of the mountains which I will tell thee of.*" God commanded that he go into the land of Moriah, and there He would direct him to which mountain to climb with his only son, Isaac. God by His foreknowledge knew that Isaac would be offered where His temple would one day be built in the future city of Jerusalem; and one day His Own Son would be offered for the sins of His people. Abraham lived somewhere near Beersheba, about 30 miles from his destination.

Verse 4: Then on the third day Abraham lifted up his eyes, and saw the place afar off.

Verse 5: And Abraham said unto his young men, Abide ye here with the ass; and I and the lad will go yonder and worship, and come again to you.

On the third day the mountains we seen: Abraham knew he and his only son had to go the rest of the way alone. We are not told of any conversations along the way. Volumes have been written about this particular scene in God's fulfillment of His plan for Redemption. Isaac in type is none other than the Son of God, who was raised from the dead on the third day, and restored to the Father with the glory they had before the world was.

Verse 6: And Abraham took the wood of the burnt offering, and laid it upon Isaac his son; and he took the fire in his hand, and a knife; and they went both of them together.

Verse 7: And Isaac spake unto Abraham his father, and said, My father: and he said, Here am I, my son. And He said, Behold the fire and the wood: but where is the lamb for a burnt offering?

Isaac had willingly followed his father every step of the way, not only from their home, but right to the top of the mountain of sacrifice. Though Isaac is called a lad, he was close to 30 years old by now. He was silent until they started the long climb, then he questioned his father: *"Where is the Lamb?"* It is possible that Isaac thought they would buy a lamb somewhere along the way; time was running out.

Verse 8: And Abraham said, My son, God will provide himself a lamb for a burnt offering: so they went both of them together.

Verse 9: And they came to the place which God had told him of; and Abraham built an altar there, and laid the wood in order, and bound Isaac his son, and laid him on the altar upon the wood.

Abraham never doubted that God would make a way. He had already told the young men at the bottom of the mountain that they would both return after they had worshipped. In Hebrews 11:17-19, we read of the New Testament account of this incident: *"By faith Abraham, when he was tried, offered up Isaac: and he that had received the promises offered up his only begotten son, Of whom it was said, That in Isaac shall thy seed be called: Accounting that God was able to raise him up even from the dead; from whence also he received him in a figure."*

Verse 10: And Abraham stretched forth his hand, and took the knife to slay his son.

The Holy Spirit led Abraham step by step. He took his journey; he took his only son; he went to the designated mountain; he built an altar; he laid the wood; he bound his son; he raised the knife to slay his son. The Angel of the Lord called unto him, and told him not to lay his hand upon Isaac. Abraham had proven to the world that he would have followed the voice of the Lord all the way. In James 2:21-24, we read that by his works Abraham was justified: *"Was not Abraham our father justified by works, when he had offered Isaac his son upon the altar? Seest thou how faith wrought with his works, and by works was faith made perfect? And the Scripture was fulfilled which saith, Abraham believed God, and it was imputed unto him for righteousness: and he was called the Friend of God. Ye see then how that by works a man is justified, and not by faith only."*

Abraham lifted up his eyes and saw a ram caught in a thicket by his horns, and he offered it to the Lord for a burnt offering.

Verse 14: And Abraham called the name of that place Jehovah-Jireh: as it is said to this day, In the mount of the Lord it shall be seen.

The Angel of the Lord called a second time from heaven and confirmed the covenant between God and Abraham. In verse 16: *"By myself have I sworn . . ."* In verse 17: *"In blessing I will bless thee, in multiplying I will multiply they seed . . ."* In verse 18: *"In thy seed shall all the nations of the earth be blessed . . ."* And Abraham returned from his place of worship with Isaac, his son. They went together to Beersheba. And Abraham dwelt at Beersheba.

After their "mountain-top" experience, Abraham and Isaac returned to the young men, as he had promised, and they headed for their home.

When Sarah was 127 years old, she died in Hebron in the land of Canaan; Abraham purchased a piece of land in Machpela, and there he buried his beloved wife. We are to note that Abraham moved around, and at this time Hebron was his home.

Sarah was the first in the patriarchal family line to die in the land of Canaan. Abraham did not own one plot of land, though God had promised it to him. He would not have a rented grave, and he insisted that he pay the full price for her grave. In Hebrews we read, *"By faith, he sojourned in the land of promise, as in a strange country, dwelling in tabernacles with Isaac and Jacob, the heirs with him of the same promise: For he looked for a city which hath foundations, whose builder and maker is God" (Hebrews 11:9-10).*

Abraham offers up Isaac
(Genesis 22:8)
"And Abraham said, my son, God will provide Himself a lamb . . ."

*Modern day Jerusalem Dome of the Rock in clear view
is traditionally the site where Isaac was offered.
(Land of Moriah).*

16.   A BRIDE FOR ISAAC
(Genesis 24-25)   (1830 B.C.)

Chapter 24 is not only the longest chapter in Genesis, it is also the greatest love story in the Bible. Man's total redemption is beautifully foreshadowed in the story of Isaac. We see Abraham as the loving father (king) who would make a marriage feast for his son. In Matthew 22:1-3 we read, *"And Jesus answered and spoke unto them again by parables, and said, The kingdom of heaven is like a certain king, who made a marriage for his son, And sent forth his servants to call them that were bidden to the wedding; and they would not come."*

The unnamed servant is a type of the Holy Spirit who does not speak of himself, but takes of the things of the Bridegroom with which to win the bride. He serves as a type of the Spirit enriching the bride with the Bridegroom's gifts. These gifts are for the homeward journey. The servant is also a type of the Spirit bringing the bride to a meeting with her Bridegroom.

In John 14, we read that the Bridegroom has gone to prepare a place for His Bride, and He promised to come again and receive her unto Himself. In verse 26, He is said to be her comforter until His return. The Spirit (Comforter) will take care of her, protect her, give gifts unto her, and teach her of her soon-coming Bridegroom.

In the story of Isaac, the servant sought out the bride for his master; he told her about her Bridegroom, and let her make the choice whether she cared to join him. He gave her gifts as they traveled on to meet Isaac (type of Christ). John 14:26 says,

"But the Comforter, which is the Holy Ghost, whom the Father will send in my name, he shall teach you all things, and bring all things to your remembrance, whatsoever I have said unto you." In John 15:26, we read, *"But when the Comforter is come whom I will send unto you from the Father, even the Spirit of truth, which proceedeth from the Father, he shall testify of me:"* Then in John 16:13-14, we read, *"Howbeit when he, the Spirit of truth, is come, he will guide you into all truth: for he shall not speak of himself; but whatsoever he shall hear, that shall he speak: and he will show you things to come. He shall glorify me: for he shall receive of mine, and shall show it unto you."* Rebekah is a type of the Church, the ecclesia, "the called out" virgin bride of Christ who loves Him before she sees Him, because of the testimony of the servant, (the Holy Spirit).

By now Abraham was well stricken in years, and he was concerned about the marriage of his only son. The Lord had fulfilled His promises to Abraham, and blessed him in all things. The following presents a very solemn time in the life of Abraham. Isaac is at least 40 years old, and it was time for him to start his own family.

Verse 2: And Abraham said unto his eldest servant of his house, that ruled over all that he had, Put, I pray thee thy hand under my thigh:

Verse 3: And I will make thee swear by the Lord, the God of heaven, and the God of the earth, that thou shalt not take a wife unto my son of the daughters of the Canaanites, among whom I dwell.

Verse 4: But thou shalt go unto my country, and to my kindred, and take a wife unto my son Isaac.

The most intelligent and faithful servant in the household was appointed overseer of the other. The word "eldest" is not of necessity speaking of age, but of authority. This was the head servant, chief of all the rest. In a similar way we use the word "elder" in an official sense, even when applied to young men. One translation uses the word "heir". This takes us back in our study to the time when Abraham fell on his face before the Lord and said, Lord God, what wilt thou give me, seeing I go childless, and the steward of my house is this Eliezer of Damascus" (Genesis 15:2)? In other words, Lord, the only heir I see right now is this steward in my household. If Eliezer were still living, he no doubt was the messenger; we are not sure since the Holy Spirit chose to leave this man nameless.

Canaan is a type of our heavenly calling. Isaac never left his homeland though others did. Canaan also typifies our warfare is no longer with flesh and blood, but with the wicked spirits in high places. places.

Abraham placed his servant under firm oath to follow his command. The servant asked of his master what he should do if the young girl would not make the long trip back with him. He wondered if he would then be required to take Isaac to her. Abraham was adamant in his reply. Under no circumstances was he to allow Isaac to go into the land of his relatives.

101

Verse 7: The Lord God of heaven, which took me from my father's house, and from the land of my kindred, and which spake unto me, and that sware unto me, saying, Unto thy seed will I give this land; he shall send his angel before thee, and thou shalt take a wife unto my son from thence.

Verse 8: And if the woman will not be willing to follow thee, then thou shalt be clear from this my oath: only bring not my son thither again.

The servant sware unto his lord, and set out upon his journey with ten camels (number of redemption), for a 500 mile journey into Mesopotamia (Iraq), the city of Nahor; for the wife of Isaac was not to be taken from the Canaanites. The long trek northward came to an end at the edge of the city by a well. He caused the camels to kneel while he sought the Lord for further directions in behalf of his master. While he was yet speaking with the Lord, a beautiful, young girl, Rebekah, (captivating) arrived at the well with a water jug on her shoulder.

The servant knew that the women of the place would come out to the wells to draw water for their households in the early evening, and this seemed a likely place to meet the right one for Isaac. One might notice that the servant's prayer took on the form of a fleece unto the Lord. He told the Lord he would stand by the well, and the girl that was the right one would come to the well, and he would ask her for water; she would not only offer water to him, but she would also offer water to the camels. It would take at least 200 gallons of water to fill 10 camels! Also, let us be reminded that the camels were heavily ladden with gifts for the bride.

Verse 16: And the damsel was very fair to look upon, a virgin, neither had any man known her: and she went down to the well, and filled her pitcher, and came up."

Verse 17: And the servant ran to meet her, and said, Let me, I pray thee, drink a little water of thy pitcher.

Verse 18: And she said, Drink, my lord: and she hasted, and let down her pitcher upon her hand, and gave him drink.

Verse 19: And when she had done giving him drink, she said, I will draw water for thy camels also, until they have done drinking.

Verse 20: And she hasted, and emptied her pitcher into the trough, and ran again unto the well to draw water, and drew for all his camels.

Verse 21: And the man wondering at her held his peace, to wit whether the Lord had made his journey prosperous or not.

He watched her carefully to see if she would do as she had said. When the camels had finished drinking, he produced a quarter-ounce gold ring and two five-ounce golden bracelets for her wrists. In the King James translation the word is "earring" which is incorrect. This was a gold ring for the nose. Rebekah ran home to tell her family about their visitor from afar. When Laban saw the ring, and the bracelets on her wrists, and heard the story, he rushed to the well to invite the servant to lodge with them. It must be noted that the first encounter we have with Laban, we are told "when he saw the ring, and the bracelets . . ." indicating that he was quite impressed with Abraham's wealth. In the life of Jacob we meet up with him again, but in full color.

The servant of Abraham bowed in an attitude of praise and worship, for he knew God had heard his prayer, and had honored his master. He thanked the Lord that he had found the bride for Isaac. Actually, he prostrated himself before the Lord which is still a Jewish custom, since to bow the knee is a sign of idolatry.

When the servant was taken into the home of Laban and Rebekah, we read of the immense prosperity of Abraham. When Abraham was called of God from Ur of the Chaldees, to go into the land of Canaan, it has already been pointed out that he was even then a wealthy man. When he faced famine in Canaan, and slipped off down into Egypt, he came out with his wealth increased greatly. We learned from Abraham's experiences that God will bless His children even in famine. In Genesis 13:2, we read, *"And Abram was very rich in cattle, in silver, and in gold."* In light of those scriptures, as we read our next text, we learn that God had consistently increased the prosperity of Abraham.

Verse 35: And the Lord hath blessed my master greatly; and he is become great: and he hath given him flocks, and herds, and silver, and gold, and menservants, and maidservants, and camels, and asses.

One translation says that God overwhelmed him with riches. In Proverbs 13:22, we are told that the wealth of the sinner is just waiting for us to claim it: *"A good man leaveth an inheritance to his children's children: and the wealth of the sinner is laid up for the just."*

The servant of Abraham recounted his exciting mission to Rebekah's family; he refused to eat with them until the matter of a bride for Isaac was settled. As soon as the agreement was made for Rebekah to become the wife of Isaac, the servant fell again to his knees before God. Then he brought out jewels set in solid gold, silver and lovely clothing for her; he gave beautiful gifts to her family. They requested that the young girl be allowed to stay at least 10 more days with them before she left her home, to which the servant replied:

Verse 56: And he said to them, Hinder me not, seeing the Lord hath prospered my way: send me away that I may go to my master.

We must note the business-like manner in which this servant handled the affairs of his master. He was eager to get back home; after all, he had a long trip ahead of him, and other matters to handle for Abraham. He was probably concerned about the length of days his master had left. The Holy Spirit will not tarry, because He knows and follows God's timetable.

Verse 60: And they bless Rebekah, and said unto her, Thou art our sister, be thou the mother of thousands of millions, and let thy seed possess the gate of those which hate them.

Verse 61: And Rebekah arose, and her damsels, and they rode upon the camels, and followed the man: and the servant took Rebekah, and went his way.

As one writer said, the grace of God is irresistible. When He moved to accomplish His eternal purpose, everything gives way before him. The natural heart must yield, as well as the renewed heart. God reached down in grace for Rebekah, even as He had previously called Abraham; and He moved her people to let her go. Flesh wants to procrastinate and keep the spirit from moving.

In the prophecy they blessed her, and asked that she become the mother of millions; and that her descendants would overcome all her enemies.

The Comforter (Paraclete) the One called alongside of, escorted the bride over long, hot, hard trails, and at the end of the journey he presented her to her husband. Over miles and miles of travel, he must have told her all about Isaac. She knew that he was waiting to welcome her home. Rebekah was the chaste bride (II Corinthians 11:2), preparing to meet her Bridegroom (John 3:29, Romans 7:4). There are several ways that Rebekah typifies the Christian believer. Her marriage was planned long before she knew about it, (Ephesians 1:3, 4); she had a part in fulfilling God's eternal purpose, (Ephesians 1:23); she was to share in the glory and the wealth of the son, (John 17:22, 23); she learned of the son through His emissary and her comforter; she immediately left all to go to the son, and she loved him before she saw him.

ISAAC LIFTED UP HIS EYES

Isaac who lived in the Negev, (the South Country), had returned to Beer-lahai-roi (Him that liveth and seeth me); he went at eventide into the field to meditate, and he lifted up his eyes and saw the camels coming. In John 17:1-2, we read, *"These words spake Jesus, and lifted up his eyes to heaven, and said, Father, the hour is come;*

glorify thy Son, that thy Son also may glorify thee."

Verse 64: And Rebekah lifted up her eyes, and when she saw Isaac, she lighted off the camel.

Verse 65: For she had said unto the servant, What man is this that walketh in the field to meet us? And the servant had said, It is my master therefore, she took a veil, and covered herself.

Verse 66: And the servant told Isaac all things that he had done.

Verse 67: And Isaac brought her into his mother Sarah's tent, and took Rebekah, and she became his wife; and he loved her: and Isaac was comforted after his mother's death.

She became his wife. *"This is a great mystery; but I speak concerning Christ and the church" (Ephesians 5:32).* Our personal relationship with our Lord is one of the most amazing truths in all the Bible. He loved her. Christ's love for His church is eternal. It was His love that brought Him down to earth to redeem her.

Isaac, like Christ:

(1) Was promised long before his coming (Luke 1:70)
(2) Finally appeared at the appointed time (Galatians 4:4)
(3) Conceived and born miraculously (Luke 1:35)
(4) Named before his birth (Matthew 1:21)
(5) Was offered up in sacrifice by his father (I John 2:2)
(6) Was obedient unto death (Philippians 2:8)
(7) Brought back from the dead (Ephesians 1:19-23)
(8) To be the head of a great nation, and bless all people

NOTE: There are two Hebrew words used for our word "virgin" and both are used of Rebekah, and both are used 2000 years later speaking of the virgin Mary. In verse 16, Rebekah is called a virgin (Bethulah). In verses 43, she is called a virgin, but another Hebrew word is used, *(almah).* The difference in the meaning of those two words has caused the skeptic to declare this to mean a young woman conceived and brought forth a son. In Isaiah 7:14, we read, "*. . . Behold, a virgin (almah) shall conceive and shall bear a son . . .*" When Rebekah came to draw water the word "bethulah" is used of her. Later, she is called "almah," because she is now a chaste virgin bethrothed to Isaac. She has the ring in her nose. With Mary, "almah" was used for the same reason. She was espoused to Joseph, but she was nevertheless, a virgin.

Abraham was 140 years old when Isaac married Rebekah. In chapter 25 we are told that he gave all that he had to Isaac though he had married Keturah, and had more sons by her. At the age of 175 he died.

Verse 5: And Abraham gave all that he had unto Isaac.

Verse 8: Then Abraham gave up the ghost, and died in a good old age, an old man, full of years; and was gathered to his people.

Verse 9: And his sons Isaac and Ishmael buried him in the cave of Machpelah, in the field of Ephron the son of Zohar the Hittite, which is before Mamre.

Abraham was buried near his wife, Sarah. After the death of his father, Isaac began to prosper and God was with him to bless him in all that he did.

Verse 11: And it came to pass after the death of Abraham, that God blessed his son Isaac; and Isaac dwelt by the well Lahai-roi.

We are reminded that Lahai-roi was Hagar's well, (Genesis 16:14; 25:11). By the time of Abraham's death, Ishmael's twelve sons were grown, and they had become prolific and powerful enough to have settled towns and reputations of their own. Then at the age of 137, Ishmael died. God had fulfilled his promise to Hagar.

Verse 21: And Isaac entreated the Lord for his wife, because she was barren: and the Lord was entreated of him, and Rebekah his wife conceived.

During her pregnancy it seemed as if she had a war going on inside of her. Rebekah sought the Lord about it; He told her she had two rival nations in her womb. He told her one would be stronger than the other, and the older would be a servant of the younger.

Verse 25: And the first came out red, all over like a hairy garment; and they called his name Esau.

Verse 26: And after that came his brother out, and his hand took hold on Esau's heel; and his name was called Jacob: and Isaac was three-score years old when she bare them.

Esau was a cunning hunter, a man of the field; but Jacob was a plain man, dwelling in tents. Isaac loved Esau, and Rebekah loved Jacob.

"And Isaac brought her into his mother Sarah's tent, and took Rebekah, and she became his wife; and he loved her: and Isaac was comforted after his mother's death" (Genesis 24:67).

Modern street scene in Israel almost identical to Bibical times.

"And it came to pass, when Jacob saw Rachel. Jacob went near, and rolled the stone from the well's mouth, and watered the flock of Laban his mother's brother"
(Genesis 29:10).

In Psalm 23 when David said, ". . . my cup runneth over . . ." he was using the idea of the cup or stone on top of the wells from which they watered their sheep in those days. (Cup or stone was too heavy for one person to lift.)

17. THE STOLEN BIRTHRIGHT
(Genesis 26-27)   (1730 B.C.)

As we view this next major section of the development of the Hebrew nation, we must remember that Jacob is the object of God's election, and so are the Jewish people. In chapter 25:29, we have the beginning of Jacob's deceit that would lead him down a trail of heartache for some twenty years.

The word "pottage" is not in the original, so when Esau came in from the field, he actually said to Jacob who had prepared the stew, "Feed me with the same red." From this came his name, "Edom." Jacob's quick reply reveals a premeditated scheme to deceive his brother and take his birthright and blessing. This is not hard to understand when we look back in our studies and see that God said the twins were struggling against one another in the womb; *"Sell me this day thy birthright,"* proves that Jacob had been listening when old Isaac talked about the blessings and promises that God had made to grandfather Abraham. Today, more people need to study the Word and know the blessings and prosperity that God has promised to us, because we are the spiritual seed of Abraham. All he inherited is ours through our birthright in the Lord Jesus Christ and by the Blood of the Lamb. Unless one comes face to face with the total sovereignty of Almight God, there will remain a mind full of questions as to the justice in choice. God had already told Rebekah His choice in a most specific way. In those days the first born automatically received the greatest honor in a family, and was looked up to; he was the one who kept the family going after the death of the parents. Our Lord God is not capricious and always has reason for what He does. The way we clear the "tabs" in our thinking is by trusting the God who created us.

Esau claimed he was at the point of death from starvation, and questioned what good was a birthright to a dying man. He agreed to make the trade. Jacob sought a good thing in the wrong way. He stands without excuse. Esau had agreed with Satan to help thwart the ways of God. God makes His plans according to His foreknowledge, and judges in light of eternity. Even in this the Lord was leading us towards the fulfillment of Genesis 3:15.

"Known unto God are all his works, from the beginning of the world" (Acts 15:18). In Romans 13:1-2, we read, *"Let every soul be subject unto the higher powers. For there is no power but of God: the powers that be are ordained of God. Whosoever therefore resisteth the power, resisteth the ordinance of God: and they that resist shall receive to themselves damnation."* In Proverbs 16:33, we are told, *"The lot is cast into the lap; but the whole disposing thereof is of the lord."* We are to learn to trust in the Lord with our very being, and lean not to our own understanding. Jacob was trying to help God for had not his mother told him of the struggle within her before his birth? Esau was "a cunning hunter," and so was Nimrod! The fact that Esau was even willing to consider selling his birthright speaks of what was in his heart.

The name Esau means "hairy" and Jacob means "heel-cathcher or supplanter." Though Isaac loved Esau, and Rebekah was partial to Jacob, God had Himself chosen Jacob to become the father of the twelve tribes of Israel. Translators call Jacob a "plain" man, or a "quiet" man, but the Hebrew word is *"tam,"* and it means "perfect" or "complete-mature." The Holy Spirit used that same word in Job 1:8, when He spoke of Job as being a "perfect-upright" man before God.

There are three elements to be considered in the birthright: (1) Until the coming of the Aaronic priesthood the head of the family exercised priestly rights; (2) The Abrahamic family held the Edenic promise of the Satan-Bruiser of Genesis 3:15, (3) Esau was in the direct line for the birthright and blessing, but God never intended that it should come through him. God can bypass all traditional values to establish His covenant in this earth.

When we consider a man who was willing to reject his birthright, and forfeit his blessings for a pot of lentils, we thank God for His wisdom and foreknowledge. He sware . . . he sold . . . he ate and drank . . . he rose up and went his willful way.

Does this not prove over and over that natural man has no heart for the things of God? We have all gone our own way and rejected His love and mercy. Jesus was the promised Seed, and God would let nothing man could devise keep Him from bringing the Redeemer to us. In Hebrews 12:16-17, we read, *"Lest there by any fornicator, or profane person, as Esau, who for one morsel of meat sold his birthright. For ye know how that afterward, when we would have inherited the blessing, he was rejected."*

Verse 1: And there was a famine in the land, beside the first famine that was in the days of Abraham. And Isaac went unto Abimelech king of the Philistines unto Gerar.

Verse 2: And the Lord appeared unto him and said, Go not down into Egypt; dwell in the land which I shall tell thee of.

Verse 3: Sojourn in this land, and I will be with thee, and will bless thee; for unto thee, and unto thy seed, I will give all these countries, and I will perform the oath which I sware unto Abraham thy father;

Verse 4: And I will make thy seed to multiply as the stars of heaven, and will give unto thy seed all these countries; and in thy seed shall all the nations of the earth be blessed;

Verse 5: Because that Abraham obeyed my voice, and kept my charge, my commandments, my statutes, and my laws.

Gerar is the borderland midway between Canaan and Egypt. This is a type of the believer out of harmony with the ways and purposes of God. There was a famine in the land just like the famine that had been in Abraham's day. King Abimelech was an old man by now for he was king in the days of Abraham. Isaac got as far as Gerar, and the Lord stopped him and confirmed the Abrahamic covenant, and promised to prosper him. God does not want us to turn to the world for help when things get rough for us. Every true child of God will be tested to prove what is in his heart. It will serve to prove our level of faith in God and His word. In I Peter 1:6-7 we read, *"Wherein ye greatly rejoice, though now for a season, if need be, ye are in heaviness through manifold temptations: That the trial of your faith, being much more precious than of gold that perisheth, though it be tried with fire, might be found unto praise and honour and glory at the appearing of Jesus Christ."* God expects His children to rejoice, and fear not. James 1:2-8 explains how we are to view trials, *". . . count it all joy when ye fall into divers temptations; . . . the trying of your faith worketh patience (endurance). But let patience have her perfect work, that ye may be perfect and entire, wanting nothing. If any of you lack wisdom, let him ask of God, that giveth to all men liberally, and upbraideth not; and it shall be given him. But let him ask in faith, nothing wavering. For he that wavereth is like a wave of the sea driven with the wind and tossed. For let not that man think that he shall receive any thing of the Lord. A double minded man is unstable in all his ways."*

History truly does repeat itself. In this text we read where Isaac repeated the same mistake his father had made by lying about his wife. In the garden Adam blamed his wife for the fall; in the life of both Abraham and Isaac, they hid behind their wives to save their own skin instead of believing God for the protection He had promised to them. Recorded history has never tried to hide the mistakes and sins of the men with which God cut covenant. All that man is, only tends to magnify the goodness and mercy of the Lord.

When the men in Gerar asked about Rebekah, he said that she was his sister. Later King Abimelech looked out his window and saw Isaac and Rebekah together, and he knew Isaac had lied to him. He called him in and demanded an answer. Abimelech took the incident quite seriously, and posted a public proclamation that anyone harming Rebekah would be killed.

Verse 12: Then Isaac sowed in that land, and received in the same year an hundredfold: and the Lord blessed him.

Verse 13: And the man waxed great, and went forward, and grew until he became very great:

Verse 14: For he had possession of flocks, and possession of herds, and great store of servants: and the Philistines envied him.

Not only did Isaac have all that Abraham had given to him, but he sowed in the land and in one year God had blessed him one-hundred fold for his labor. The Philistines were jealous of him. God wants the world to be jealous of His children. The covenant promises were made to Abraham (man of the altar), repeated to Isaac, (man of wells), and to Jacob (man of tents). This covenant was ratified by sacrifice, and confirmed by Divine Oath. What God had promised, He would perform. In a time of desolating famine, Isaac had the covenant promises renewed to him. Perhaps this was his time of greatest need. Based upon the covenant God had made with Abraham, Isaac had a three-fold promise:

(1) A promise of Divine Presence, *"I will be thee."*
(2) A promise of blessing, *"I will bless thee."*
(3) A promise of territory, *"I will give thee all these countries.*

117

Isaac redug the wells of his father, Abraham. These wells had been filled with dirt after his father's death. His shepherds also dug a well in Gerar Valley, and found a gushing underground spring. These are the names of the wells, (1) Lahai-roi-"Him that liveth and seeth me," for Isaac came from the way of the well, (2) Esek-"Contention," (3) Sitnah-"Hatred," (4) Rehoboth-"Room," (5) Shebah-"Well of the Oath."

When Isaac went to Beersheba, the Lord appeared to him and said:

Verse 24: And the Lord appeared unto him the same night, and said, I am the God of Abraham thy father: fear not, for I am with thee, and will bless thee, and multiply thy seed for my servant Abraham's sake.

Verse 25: And he builded an altar there, and called upon the name of the Lord, and pitched his tent there: and there Isaac's servants digged a well.

King Abimelech paid him a visit to make peace since he had asked Isaac to leave Gerar. Isaac made a feast for them, and they took solemn oaths to live in peace with one another. The same day Isaac's men hit another gusher. This he named the **WELL OF THE OATH,** and the city that grew up there was called by that name.

STOLEN BLESSING

Esau was forty years old when he took Judith, and Basemath (Hittites) for his wives. Isaac was old in years, and when it came time to bless his sons, he made a last request of Esau. He wanted venison, his favorite food, to be prepared for him before his death.

Rebekah overheard the conversation between Isaac and Esau, and she called Jacob to her. One is not to view this as a "spur-of-the-moment" idea on the part of Rebekah. Had not God told her from their conception, that the younger would rule? She pledged in her heart to help God. Little did she know that her sin would drive her favorite son from her side, and that she would never again see him in the flesh. Isaac set about to deliberately disobey God by blessing his firstborn after he had eaten meat. Rebekah sent Jacob out to get two young goats for her to substitute for the venison he had requested. She had it all planned out. In verse 10, we read, *"And thou shalt bring it to thy father, that he may eat, and that he may bless thee before his death."* As soon as Jacob brought the two kids to his mother, she prepared a delicious meal for Isaac. She had thought of everything. She took Esau's best clothes and put them on Jacob. They had the smell of the field to them: She made Jacob gloves from the hairy skin of the young goats, and fastened some of the hide around his neck; then she sent Jacob to the bedside of Isaac who was nearly blind.

"I am Esau thy firstborn . . ."

"How did you find the meat so soon?"

"Your God was with me."

"Come near, my son, that I may feel . . . art thou my   son, Esau?"

"I am."

119

Bring the food near me. I will eat. Then I will bless thee ... come near and kiss me ... he smelled ... he blessed ... yes, it is the smell of the field ... therefore, God give thee of dew of heaven, and the fatness of the earth, and the plenty of corn and wine: Let people serve thee, and nations bow to thee: be lord over thy brethren, and let thy mother's sons bow down to thee: cursed be every one that curseth thee, and blessed be he that blesseth thee." Jacob had scarcely left the room, when his brother, Esau, came in and discovered what had happened to his blessing.

Verse 35: Thy brother came with subtlety, and hath taken away thy blessing. Esau cried out that Jacob had taken away his birthright and now he had stolen his blessing.

And Esau hated Jacob because of the blessing. He vowed that he would slay Jacob as soon as the traditional mourning period had ended after Isaac's death.

Rebekah was told, and she sent Jacob to her relatives in Padan-aram, to take a wife from her brother, Laban. She thought Jacob would stay there for a few days, then she would send for him when Esau's anger had abated. This was her scheming way of getting Jacob out of the house to safety.

Verse 46: And Rebekah said to Isaac, I am weary of my life because of the daughters of Heth: if Jacob take a wife of the daughters of Heth, such as these which are the daughters of the land, what good shall my life do me?

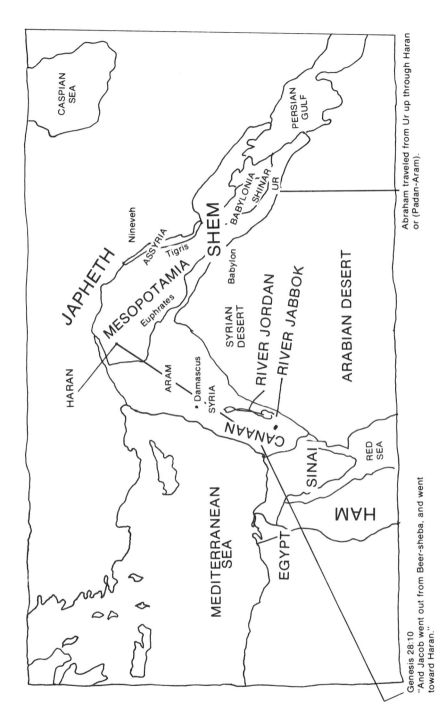

CASPIAN SEA

PERSIAN GULF

Abraham traveled from Ur up through Haran or (Padan-Aram).

Nineveh

JAPHETH

ASSYRIA

Tigris

SHEM

BABYLONIA

SHINAR

UR

MESOPOTAMIA

Euphrates

Babylon

HARAN

ARAM

Damascus

SYRIA

SYRIAN DESERT

RIVER JORDAN

RIVER JABBOK

CANAAN

ARABIAN DESERT

SINAI

RED SEA

MEDITERRANEAN SEA

EGYPT

HAM

Genesis 28:10
"And Jacob went out from Beer-sheba, and went toward Haran."

121

18. BETHEL-HOUSE OF GOD (Bread)
(Genesis 28)   (1730 B.C.)

Verse 1: And Isaac called Jacob, and blessed him, and charged him, and said unto him, thou shalt not take a wife of the daughters of Canaan.

Verse 2: Arise, go to Padan-aram, to the house of Bethuel thy mother's father; and take thee a wife from thence from the daughter of Laban thy mother's brother.

Verse 3: And God Almighty bless thee, and make thee fruitful, and multiply thee, that thou mayest be a multitude of people;

Verse 4: And give thee the blessing of Abraham, to thee, and to thy seed with thee; that thou mayest inherit the land wherein thou art a stranger, which God gave unto Abraham.

Jacob obeyed his father and mother, and left home for his mother's people. Just as the sun set, he stopped to make camp for the night. He took a few stones and made himself a pillow. He lay down to sleep, and God visited him in a dream.

STAIRWAY TO HEAVEN

Verse 12: And he dreamed, and behold a ladder set up on the earth, and the top of it reached to heaven: and behold the angels of God ascending and descending on it.

Verse 13: And, behold, the Lord stood above it, and said, I am the Lord God of Abraham thy father, and the God of Isaac: the land whereon thou liest, to thee will I give it, and to thy seed;

Verse 14: And thy seed shall be as the dust of the earth, and thou shalt spread abroad to the west, and to the east, and to the north, and to the south: and in thee and in thy seed shall all the families of the earth be blessed.

Verse 15: And, behold, I am with thee and will keep thee in all places whither thou goest, and will bring thee again into this land; for I will not leave thee, until I have done that which I have spoken to thee of.

When Jacob arrived at Bethel, he was about 75 miles north of Beersheba, and had possibly traveled some three to four days. When the translators say, *"he lighted upon a certain place,"* it sounds as if he arrived at Bethel quite by accident, but God does not lead people by "chance." He charts a deliberate course for each of us, for it is not possible that man can know his way. In Jeremiah 10:23 we read, *"O Lord, I know the way of man is not in himself: it is not in man that walketh to direct his steps."*

It was near Bethel that Abraham had built an altar (Genesis 12:8; 13:3, 4), and Jacob would return to this place years later. Over a thousand years later, this place was totally destroyed because of apostasy. (I Kings 12:28: 33; II Kings 23: 15-17).

Quite obviously, this was no ordinary ladder. It began on earth and reached far into heaven. It was wide and high. The angels of God were ascending and descending during the course of this dream. Not only does this present to us the ministry of angels as messengers for the Lord, but they are ministering spirits for the heirs of salvation: In

Hebrews 1:14 we read, *"Are they not all ministering spirits, sent forth to minister for them who shall be heirs of salvation?"*

The ladder was symbolic of man's link with God, through the Lord Jesus Christ. *"And he saith unto him, Verily, verily, I say unto you, Hereafter ye shall see heaven open, and the angels of God ascending and descending upon the Son of Man" (John 1:51).* God did not rebuke Jacob, but gave him a review of the blessings that He had promised to Abraham which would be fulfilled in him. God knew that if Jacob walked by sight, appearances would contradict the promises He had made. In that lonely, deserted place, God renewed His covenant with the grandson of Abraham. Jacob saw the angels; he saw God standing at the top of the ladder to bring comfort to Jacob's heart. He promised never to leave him, and that he would never leave him. In Hebrews 13:5 we are given this same assurance under the new covenant, *"... I will never leave thee, nor forsake thee."*

The life of Jacob serves as a perfect example of how God overrules our folly and weaknesses, and though we reap what we sow, He uses each setback to teach us of His own tender love and perfect wisdom in all things. We are commanded to trust Him, and our failures are often the cause for much regret later. God is the only One who can bring good out of evil.

When Jacob woke up, he exclaimed, *"God is really in this place."* Early the next morning, he set his stone headrest upright as a memorial to what had happened there. He poured olive oil over it, and named the place *"House of God"* or Beth-el. It was first called Luz. Later on the city of Luz moved on up north. It was then that Jacob made his vow to God. The word "if" should have been translated "since." Jacob was not making a deal with God, though some have claimed this was beautifully in keeping with his name "supplanter." Jacob was awestruck by this experience. He vowed a vow unto the Lord that since He had appeared to him, and renewed His promises, he would always be his God, and he would return unto the Lord one tenth of all he possessed. Since oil is a type of the Holy Spirit, Jacob was anointing and consecrating that spot as a place of dedication and worship. Should he forget in days or even years to come the experience of that place, he would have to return and renew his vows before God. (This is the first mention of the use of oil poured upon an altar.)

Jacob's Ladder
"And, behold, the Lord stood above it . . ." (Genesis 28:13).

126

19. JACOB AND LABAN
(Genesis 29-31)

Genesis 29 through 31 is the story of Jacob's twenty long years away from Canaan, his home. He was close to 75 years old when he left home, so he would be 95 upon his return. These proved to be very happy and prosperous years, although his dealings with Laban might lead one to believe he was reaping the bitter seeds of his past. It might well be remembered that God had met him on his way to the land of the children of the East, and He had renewed all the promises that He had made with Abraham, Isaac, and now Jacob. He had ample reason to "lift up his feet" and finish his journey with sheer joy in his heart. God had promised to prosper him in all his ways.

As Jacob neared his goal, the town of Haran in Mesopotamia, God guided him to the very spot where he would meet Rachel as she watered her father's flock. He saw in the distance three flocks of sheep lying beside a well in an open field, waiting to be watered. It was their custom to wait until all the flocks were gathered before they rolled the stone from the well. The stone, or sheep's cup as it was called, was far too heavy for one person to lift from the well. It would be lifted and turned over to offer a trough in which to pour water for sheep. They are still used by the shepherds in Israel today.

Jacob did not understand why all the flocks were gathered with their shepherds at the well so early in the day; he greeted them in a friendly manner, and asked where they lived. He was as delighted as Abraham's servant when he came in search of a bride for Isaac to learn they were from Haran, and they knew Laban. As he spoke with the young men, Rachel came to the well to water her father's sheep.

Verse 10: And it came to pass, when Jacob saw Rachel the daughter of Laban his mother's brother, and the sheep of Laban his mother's brother, that Jacob went near, and rolled the stone from the well's mouth, and watered the flock of Laban his mother's brother.

Verse 11: And Jacob kissed Rachel, and lifted up his voice, and wept.

Jacob helped Rachel water Laban's flock, then he kissed her and started crying as he introduced himself as her cousin. We must note that they spoke the same language. The language of Haran was Aramaic (Chaldee) which was certainly a language well know to Abraham.

Verse 13: And it came to pass, when Laban heard the tidings of Jacob his sister's son, that he ran to meet him, and embraced him, and kissed him, and brought him to his house. And he told Laban all these things.

After a month had passed, Laban told Jacob that he wanted to pay him for his labor. Jacob, without hesitation, told Laban he wanted to serve him for seven years for the hand of Rachel. At the end of the seven years, Jacob marveled at how quickly the time had passed; it seemed so short because he was in love with beautiful Rachel.

The time had arrived for the wedding and Laban devised one of the most medacious schemes imaginable; perhaps equalled only by Jacob and Rebekah's plot to steal the birthright and blessing of Esau. Again, we must be reminded that the birthright was already Jacob's according to the Word of the Lord.

Verse 21: And Jacob said unto Laban, Give me my wife, for my days are fulfilled, that I may go in unto her.

Verse 22: And Laban gathered together all the men of the place, and made a feast.

Verse 23: And it came to pass in the evening, that he took Leah his daughter, and brought her to him; and he went in unto her.

Verse 24: And Laban gave unto his daughter Leah, Zilpah his maid, for an handmaid.

Verse 25: And it came to pass, that in the morning, behold, it was Leah: and he said to Laban, What is this thou hast done unto me? Did not I serve with thee for Rachel? wherefore then hast thou beguilded me?

Jacob was enraged by this betrayal. He had worked for seven years for the woman he loved, and had received a substitute for all his labors. Laban insisted that it simply was not their custom to marry off the youngest daughter first; He asked Jacob to wait until the bridal week was over, and he would give him Rachel also; but he had another trick "up his sleeve." Jacob would have to serve him another seven years.

Verse 29: And Laban gave to Rachel his daughter, Bilhah his handmaid, to be her maid.

Mention is made of the two maids because they would play an important part in the development of the 12 tribes of Israel. Rachel was barren, but Leah was remembered by God, and she conceived and began to give Jacob sons which caused Rachel to become intensely jealous of her.

THE TWELVE TRIBES OF ISRAEL

SONS OF LEAH

Reuben	"Behold a son"
Simeon	"Hearing"
Levi	"Joined"
Judah	"Praise"
Issachar	"Bought with a Price"
Zebulon	"Dwelling"

SON OF ZILPAH, LEAH'S MAID

Gad	"A Great Company"
Asher	"Happy, Joyous"

SONS OF RACHEL

Joseph	"Fruitful bough"
Benjamin	"Son of my Right Hand or Strength"

SONS OF BELHAH, RACHEL'S MAID

Dan	"God Will Judge"
Naphtali	"Wrestling"

NOTE: Eight hundred years before Moses, King Amraphel (Genesis 14:1) named Hammurabi promulgated a code of laws which governed the peoples from the Persian Gulf to the Caspian Sea, and from Persia to the Mediterranean. Under these laws, a woman could give her handmaid to her

130

husband to bear him children, if she proved to be barren. Since our cultures are so different from the East, it is impossible for us to imagine such a law.

Soon after the birth of his son, Joseph, Jacob told Laban that it was time for him to go back to his own country and people. Jacob was quite a wealthy man by now in his own right. Laban began to plead for him not to leave him. Laban knew that God had favored him because of the presence of Jacob. He offered him more wages if he would only stay with him.

Jacob reminded Laban of how well he had served him, and that because of his faithful service Laban's flocks and herds had grown immensely. Jacob struck up one more bargain with Laban.

Verse 31: And he said, What shall I give thee? And Jacob said, Thou shalt not give me any thing: if thou wilt do this thing for me, I will again feed and keep thy flock.

Verse 32: I will pass through all thy flock today, removing from thence all the speckled and spotted cattle, and all the brown cattle among the sheep, and the spotted and speckled among the goats: and of such shall be my hire

Verse 33: So shall my righteousness answer for me in time to come, when it shall come for my hire before thy face: every one that is not speckled and spotted among the goats, and brown among the sheep, that shall be counted stolen with me.

SPOTTED AND SPECKLED

Jacob saw an opportunity to make an even greater fortune off Laban, who had deceived him for so many years. He requested all the spotted and speckled goats, and the black sheep. To this Laban agreed. Jacob told Laban if he ever found any white goats or sheep in his flock, Laban could say they were stolen from him. On that same day Laban formed a flock for Jacob of all the male goats that were ringed and spotted, and the females that were speckled and spotted with white patches; and he gave him the black sheep. He rounded them up and gave them to Jacob's sons to take a three days' journey from Laban, and Jacob stayed behind to work.

The ringed and spotted animals were simply less desirable to Laban than the others; Jacob was trusting God for the increase though his methods might seem a bit out of the ordinary. Jacob had promised Laban that none of his flock would be used for breeding purposes. Eastern sheep are almost wholly white; the goats black; the mixed-colored are rare. This sounded like a winner to Laban. Some have suggested that Jacob was acting true to his nature by this act; but it must be remembered that Laban asked him what would be his wages, and he agreed to the bargain. Skeptics have challenged the accuracy of the Bible in regard to this story because there is no scientific evidence for such "prenatal" influence; Jacob knew nothing of science; he was simply acting upon the promises God had given him at the place called Bethel, and a dream he had during their mating season.

Verse 37: And Jacob took him rods of green poplar, and of the hazel and chestnut tree; and pilled white strakes in them, and made the white appear which was in the rods.

Verse 38: And he set the rods which he had pilled before the flocks in the gutters in the watering troughs when the flocks came to drink, that they should conceive when they came to drink.

Verse 39: And the flocks conceived before the rods, and brought forth cattle ringstraked, speckled, and spotted.

Verse 40: And Jacob did separate the lambs, and set the faces of the flocks toward the ringstraked, and all the brown in the flock of Laban; and he put his own flocks by themselves, and put them not unto Laban's cattle.

Verse 41: And it came to pass, whensoever the stronger cattle did conceive, that Jacob laid the rods before the eyes of the cattle in the gutters, that they might conceive among the rods.

Verse 42: But when the cattle were feeble, he put them not in: so the febbler were Laban's, and the stronger Jacob's.

Verse 43: And the man increased exceedingly, and had much cattle, and maidservants, and menservants, and camels, and asses.

All this was the miracle that God had promised Jacob. God performs His greatest miracles at a time when man can do nothing for himself. He will do nothing without receiving all the praise and glory for it. Man can only move in line with the spoken Word of God, and God will honor that Word.

Laban and his sons were angry with Jacob for he had taken their wealth. When Jacob saw the face of Laban, he realized it was time to head for home. The voice of God came to him telling him to return. In chapter 31 we read of God's further dealings with Jacob, and Jacob told of his dream and how the angel of the Lord had spoken to him.

Verse 3: And the Lord said unto Jacob, Return unto the land of thy fathers, and to thy kindred; and I will be with thee.

Jacob called his family together to tell them God had spoken to him, and they would have to leave soon for his home land. He told his two wives that he had worked hard for them, and had served Laban well through the years.

Verse 7: But your father hath deceived me, and changed my wages ten times; but God suffered him not to hurt me.

Verse 8: If he said thus, The speckled shall be thy wages; then all the cattle bare speckled: and if he said thus, The ringstraked shall be thy hire; then bare all the cattle ringstraked.

Verse 9: Thus God hath taken away the cattle of your father, and given them to me.

Verse 10: And it came to pass at the time the cattle conceived, that I lifted up mine eyes, and saw in a dream, and, behold, the rams which leaped upon the cattle were ringstraked, speckled, and grisled.

Verse 11: And the angel of God spake unto me in a dream, saying, Jacob: and I said, Here am I.

Verse 12: And he said, Lift up now thine eyes, and see, all the rams which leap upon the cattle are ringstraked, speckled, and grisled: for I have seen all that Laban doeth unto thee.

Verse 13: I am the God of Beth-el, where thou anointedst the pillar, and where thou vowedst a vow unto me: now arise, get thee out from this land, and return unto the land of thy kindred.

The angel of the Lord (pre-incarnate Christ) assured Jacob that it was God who had increased him mightily and not his own divining rods. *"I Am the God of Abraham, Isaac, and now I am your God."*

While Laban was gone to shear his sheep, Jacob loaded up his caravan, and headed for home. Rachel had stolen the images that belonged to Laban; they crossed the Euphrates river and headed for the land of Gilead. It was three days later than Laban learned of their flight. He took some of his men with him, and within seven days he had caught up with Jacob at Mount Gilead; but during the night God appeared to Laban in a dream and warned him not to harm Jacob nor speak either good or bad to him. Laban confronted Jacob with that "poor little me" attitude, and contended with Jacob that he had not allowed him to say goodbye to his daughters, or give a farewell party for them. He confessed to Jacob that God had warned him not to speak either good or bad against him. But he asked, *"Why have you stolen my images?"*

Jacob did not know that it was Rachel who had taken the images. He spoke a curse over her with the words of his mouth unaware of her guilt.

Verse 32: With whomsoever thou findest thy gods, let him not live: before our brethren discern thou what is thine with me, and take it to thee. For Jacob knew not that Rachel had stolen the images and had placed them in the saddle of the camel and sat upon them."

Laban searched the tents but nothing was found. She begged off being searched due to her monthly cycle. Multiplied words passed between Laban and Jacob before they finally made a covenant of peace between them. Laban spent the night then left for his own home.

Teraphim (Images)
(Genesis 31:32)
"With whomsoever thou findest thy gods, let
him not live . . ."

20. ISRAEL: A PRINCE WITH GOD
(Genesis 32-35)

Jacob left the home of his Uncle at the command of God, with Laban in hot pursuit and somewhat troubled about the attitude of his brother Esau; twenty years prior he had vowed he would kill Jacob after the death of their father. Isaac was on his death bed when Jacob fled after stealing the birthright and blessings from his brother.

Things began to look up for Jacob when Laban suggested that they sign a peace pact, promising each other they would live and abide by its terms. They gathered stones as a monument, and ate together beside it. It was called *"Jegar-sahadutha,"* in Laban's language and *"Galeed"* in Jacob's. It was also called "The Watchtower" (Mizpah). Laban and Jacob took the oath that neither would cross the line to destroy the other. Then Jacob made a sacrifice unto God at the top of the mount, and tarried there all night.

As Jacob and his household and all he possessed started homeward, the Angels of the Lord met him on the way. When Jacob saw them he knew a host of heavenly beings had been sent to guard him as he traveled towards home. God's love is like Himself; the same yesterday, today, and forever.

Verse 1: And Jacob went his way, and the angels of God met him.

Verse 2: And when Jacob saw them, he said, This is God's host: and he called the name of that place Mahanaim.

Mahanaim means "two hosts, or camps." "Esau ... Esau ... what will you do to me? When one faces the possibility of death, faith often gets pushed into the background, and the arm of flesh begins to rule the heart in fear. The angels had been sent to strengthen Jacob, and to increase his faith in God to deliver him, yet he sent messengers ahead to check out the situation he thought he was about to face. He was unwilling to lead his family into an ambush. Another test of faith! Yet, how timely are God's interventions.

The messengers returned to Jacob, and told him Esau was on his way to meet them, and he had some 400 men with him. Jacob didn't stand up firm and declare, *"I have the angels of the Lord encamped around about me."* No, he was sacred to the core. He divided his people into two camps. He thought if one got slaughtered the other could escape. It is easy to stand forth and declare undying faith and allegiance to God when things are running smoothly; but the real test is in the midst of the fiery furnace when the pressure is turned on seven times. In this scheme we have a picture of the human heart. One writer said that when our eye is full of our own management, we cannot see the hand of God moving in our behalf. Jacob managed, then prayed. Remember Laban was an enemy in the world; but Esau represented the enemy in Canaan-or the promised land.

Verse 9: And Jacob said, O God of my father Abraham, and God of my father Isaac, the Lord which saidst unto me, Return unto thy country, and to thy kindred, and I will deal well with thee:

139

Verse 10: I am not worthy of the least of all the mercies, and of all the truth, which thou hast shown unto thy servant; for with my staff I passed over this Jordan; and now I am become two bands.

Verse 11: Deliver me, I pray thee, from the hand of my brother, from the hand of Esau: for I fear him, lest he will come and smite me, and the mother with the children.

Verse 12: And thou saidst, I will surely do thee good, and make thy seed as the sand of the sea, which cannot be numbered for multitude.

After he had sought the Lord, he gathered gifts of what he had to send to Esau:

200 she goats
20 he goats
200 ewes
20 rams
30 milk camels, with colts
40 cows
10 bulls
20 female donkeys
10 male donkeys

NAME CHANGE

Jacob sent his servants ahead of him to meet his brother, and present his peace offerings to him. Jacob had poured out his heart before the Lord, so there is certainly reason to believe God spoke to his heart and told him to send his brother these gifts. Fear is not of God, but when we pray, our next move is of God. A gift is always in line either as an apology or an act of love; here it would be both. He was asking his brother for acceptance. While he was lodging that night with the company, he arose and took all his wives and children over the river Jordan at the Jabbok ford. He returned again to the camp, and was there alone when a Man wrestled with him until daybreak.

Verse 25: And when he saw that he prevailed not against him, he touched the hollow of his thigh; and the hollow of Jacob's thigh was out of joint, as he wrestled with him.

Here is Spirit wrestling with the flesh; the Man wrestled, but in the early hours of the morning, the Man used a supernatural means to conqueor Jacob.

Verse 26: And he said, Let me go, for the day breaketh. And he said, I will not let thee go, except thou bless me.

Verse 27: And he said unto him, What is thy name? And he said, Jacob.

Verse 28: And he said, Thy name shall be called no more Jacob, but Israel: for as a prince hast thou power with God and with men, and hast prevailed.

Jacob asked the Man his name. The Man answered his question with a question, which is custom with Jews.

Verse 29: And Jacob asked him, and said, Tell me, I pray thee, thy name. And he said, Wherefore is it that thou dost ask after thy name? And he blessed him there.

Verse 30: And Jacob called the name of the place Peniel: for I have seen God face to face, and my life is preserved.

Verse 31: And as he passed over Penuel the sun rose upon him, and he halted upon his thigh.

Verse 32: Therefore the children of Israel eat not of the sinew which shrank, which is upon the hollow of the thigh, unto this day: because he touched the hollow of Jacob's thigh in the sinew that shrank.

That is why the people of Israel still do not eat the sciatic muscle where it attaches to the hip. As one Jewish man said, "That is why we are not allowed to eat Porterhouse steak, T-bone steak, or New York steak."

Jacob was no longer the "supplanter." He was now the "prevailer." The name "Israel," has continued to be the name of his descendants for 3700 years, and it means "One Who Fights Victoriously With God." It is also rendered, "A Prince With God."

This was the beginning of the development of Israel under a God-given name. As Jacob limped along, it was a constant reminder that he had not dreamed, but had prevailed that night. This was an indication of his new beginning. We must note here that there were stages in the development of the Hebrew people. There were a Hebrew family; Israelitish nation; Jewish church, or in religion. (The Jews were descendants of Judah, and the Israelites were the descendants of Jacob, whose name was changed.) Both Jews and Israelites were the descendants of Abraham the Hebrew.

NOTE: Jacob had contended with Esau in the womb and had won. He had contended for the birthright and blessing, and had won. He contended with Laban and won. He contended with God and learned dependence upon God. Flesh will forever limp in the presence of Almighty God. In Hosea 12:4 we read, *"Yea, he had power over the angel, and prevailed: he wept, and made supplication unto him: he found him in Beth-el, and there he spake with us;"*

In Chapter 33:3-4, we read of Jacob and Esau reunited.

Verse 3: And he passed over before them, and bowed himself to the ground seven times, until he came near to his brother.

Verse 4: And Esau ran to meet him, and embraced him, and fell on his neck, and kissed him: and they wept."

Jacob insisted that Esau accept the gifts he had selected for him. After several refusals, he agreed. In verse 14 we view the flesh again. Jacob still had his doubts about the good intentions of his brother. O how long will the mercy of God content with us? He used the family as an excuse to get away from Esau, and told an absolute lie to him. He promised to meet him in Seir. However, Jacob had no intentions of going to Seir. In verse 15 Esau leaves 200 of his men with Jacob, and travels on to his destination. This still doesn't convince Jacob; as soon as his brother was out of sight, he headed for Succoth. There he built a house, and made booths for his cattle: therefore the name of the place is called Succoth, (or huts.) In verse 18 we read that Jacob and his family then went on to Shechem, in Canaan, and he camped outside the city. He bought the land he camped on, and there he built an altar unto the Lord and called it *"El-Elohe-Israel," "The Altar to the God of Israel."* Jacob had not been told to go to Shechem; he was not in the will of the Lord by this move. This was spiritual lapse on his part. Jacob set up his tent on the "borderline of the world." One writer said that perhaps Jacob thought to conciliate his conscience by building an altar, and dedicating it to the God of Israel. Or perhaps he thought to counteract the effect of the idolatrous city, by this means.

DINAH DEFILED

In chapter 34 the Holy Spirt has pointed out the results of living in undesirable environments. Dinah was the daughter of Leah. She was a teen-ager by now. Jacob probably had been living in either Succoth or Shechem (or both) for several years. Reuben, Simeon, and Levi were by now in their twenties. She went alone into the city, and the son of King Hamor the Hivite, raped her. He fell in love with her and asked his father to set up a marriage for him with Dinah.

When Jacob heard of the incident, he waited until his sons came in from the field to decide their next step. The brothers were grieved about their sister, and devised a scheme that would cripple the entire city. The word "vile deed" in the Hebrew means "senseless wickedness."

Hamor told Jacob that his son, Shechem, wanted to marry Dinah for he truly loved her. He further suggested that their sons and daughters begin to intermarry since they all lived in the area together. The young man pleaded on his own behalf for Dinah, but her brothers remained irate with the king's son, and all the inhabitants of the city.

Verse 14: And they said unto them, We cannot do this thing, to give our sister to one that is uncircumcised; for that were a reproach unto us:

Verse 15: But in this will we consent unto you: If ye will be as we be, that every male of you be circumcised;

Verse 16: Then will we give our daughters unto you, and we will take your daughters to us, and we will dwell with you, and we will become one people.

They used the Holy Covenant seal to strip an entire city in their anger. They would never consider intermarriage unless all the males agreed to circumcision. The king agreed. Every male was circumcised, and on the third day, when they were in severe pain, and could not defend themselves, Simeon and Levi rushed upon the city, slew all the males, including the king and his son. They took Dinah, who had stayed with Shechem willingly and the spoils of the city, and returned home.

Verse 30: And Jacob said to Simeon and Levi, Ye have troubled me to make me a stink amoung the inhabitants of the land, among the Canaanites and the Perizzites: and I being few in number, they shall gather themselves together against me; and I shall be destroyed, I and my house.

Verse 31: And they said, should he deal with our sister as with a harlot?

Jacob had left the matter in the hands of his sons, but when they came back with all the spoils of battle, he complained that they had ruined him in the eyes of the Canaanites (world). Jacob's silence regarding the rape of his only daughter is not an easy one to explain. Was he getting too old to care? Or had the fact that he himself had lived four women all these years actually deadened his feelings about such matters? Since Dinah had apparently stayed after the defilement, why all the fuss? However, his silence does not speak well of his character. There seemed to be no sense of remorse for the need to defile a city, just revenge because of wounded pride. No doubt the entire family had been dealing in the ways of the world far too long. It was time to move on.

RACHEL'S DEATH

In chapter 35 God spoke again to Jacob telling him to go back to Beth-el, the place where He had first appeared to him. The head of the family had certainly taken a back seat in the spiritual training of his children.

Verse 1: And God said, unto Jacob, Arise, go up to Beth-el, and dwell there: and make there an altar unto God, that appeared unto thee when thou fleddest from the face of Esau thy brother.

Verse 2: Then Jacob said unto his household, and to all that were with him, Put away the strange gods that are among you, and be clean, and change your garments.

146

Verse 3: And let us arise, and go up to Beth-el; and I will make there an altar unto God, who answered me in the day of my distress, and was with me in the way which I went.

Verse 4: And they gave unto Jacob all the strange gods which were in their hand, and all their earrings which were in their ears; and Jacob hid them under the oak which was by Shechem.

The fact that the name of God is not so much as mentioned in the last chapter which is full of lust, and greed, and murder, lends understanding to us as we read, *"Arise and go,"* in the chapter before us. Jacob had really settled down in the world. Some thirty years had passed since he encounted the Lord in a dream as the Angels ascended and descended on the ladder into heaven. Chapter 35 in contrast with 34 shows the longsuffering of God in His dealings with His children. Before they moved on, they buried their idols and images. Rachel must have kept her idols all those years, (teraphim) and that would certainly prove to be a snare to the entire clan. Could this be the answer to the many who have questioned the silence of Jacob in the chapter 34? Jacob knew of the idols and images that were in his own home. He knew this was an abomination to God. Yet he deliberately chose not to hassle with the family about it. One knows when he has no ground for an audience due to sin. Sin must be put away and Beth-el reclaimed. (It would be of interest to note here that thousands of baked tile tablets have been uncovered in the regions where Laban lived. The writings indicated that a son-in-law could appear in a court of law upon the death of the father-in-law and claim a large share of the inheritance if he held these particular idols. In other words, the images were his title deed to the possession.) With that in mind, it is easier to understand Rebekah's greed in regard to her father's gods.

Jacob and his family arrived safely at the town of Luz, which he had renamed Bethel, and there he built an altar and named the altar "El-Bethel," (The House of God). It was there that Rebekah's nurse died, and they buried her under the oak, (the oak of weeping). She had been with Jacob all the years that he had been gone from home. She came with Rebekah when she married Isaac. (Genesis 25:59).

GOD CONFIRMED JACOB'S NAME

Verse 10: And God said unto him, Thy name is Jacob: thy name shall not be called any more Jacob, but Israel shall be thy name: and he called his name Israel:

Verse 11: And God said unto him, I am God Almighty: be fruitful and multiply; a nation and a company of nations shall be of thee, and kings shall come out of thy loins;

Verse 12: And the land which I gave Abraham and Isaac, to thee I will give it, and to thy seed after thee will I give the land.

God Almighty (the El Shaddai) had reminded Jacob of his name change. Nations would come from his loins, and the land that God had promised to his fathers, he would give to him. God went up from Jacob, and he set up a pillar in the place where He

148

had spoken, a pillar of stone, and he poured a drink offering upon the pillar, and he poured oil thereon. The drink offering symbolized the shed blood of Jesus Christ, and the oil is a symbol of the Holy Ghost. (Wine and the oil). This is a picture of restored communion with the Father.

Jacob began his journey from Bethel toward Ephrath, the old name of Bethlehem. Rachel went into hard labor, and while she was dying she named her new born son Ben-oni or "Son of my Sorrow." Jacob renamed the baby Benjamin, or "Son of My Right Hand." (From the tribe of Benjamin came Saul of Tarsus). The place where Jacob buried his beloved wife Rachel, was about two miles from where Jesus Christ was born in the little city of Bethlehem. The male babies that Herod killed while he was trying to find the Christ Child, were said to be buried about two miles away from her grave.

Israel continued his journey and spread his tent beyond Migdal-eder. While he dwelt in that land, his son Reuben lay with Bilhah, Israel's concubine, and Israel was told about it. His sons Levi and Simeon had taken part in the massacre of Shechem, and now Reuben had sinned grievously. This ruled out Reuben the firstborn from receiving the blessing, and the birthright, and the kingship. Simeon and Levi were ruled out because of Shechem. This meant that Judah would receive the birthright, the blessing, and the kingship. From Judah (Praise) would come the Lion of the tribe of

Judah. He would receive the priesthood, the birthright, the blessing, and He would be King of kings and Lord of lords.

THE DEATH OF ISAAC

Jacob once again returned to the home of his aged father who had been on his death bed for some thirty years. At the ripe age of 180, he finally died in Hebron where Abraham, too, had lived, and Jacob and Esau buried him.

Rachel's Tomb in (Ephrath), which is Bethlehem.

Camel's Furniture
(Genesis 31:34)
"Now Rachel had taken the images, and put
them in the camel's furniture, and sat upon
them . . ."

21. JOSEPH IN EGYPT
(Genesis 37) (1699 B.C.)

COAT OF MANY COLORS

The 36th chapter of Genesis dealt with all the descendants of Esau who would be always a thorn in the side of the Jewish people. Most of the wickedness of the earth could be traced back to Esau's offspring. We encounter them in a greater extent in the book of Exodus.

Jacob finally settled in the land of his fathers, sojourning in the land of Canaan, (Hebron). Jacob had two sons, Joseph and Benjamin, by his beloved wife, Rachel. Joseph was now 17 years old and his dad's favorite. No where in all scripture can one find a more true type of Christ than in the life of Joseph. He was the object of his father's love; object of the envy of his own-in his humiliation, sufferings, death, exaltation and glory. In all, we have our Lord strikingly typified by Joseph. We have more personal details about Joseph than about any other Bible character.

All his other sons had been a source of grief to him, but Joseph, the son of his old age, gave him joy and comfort; he had put him in charge of the sons of the handmaids, though he was not yet considered of age which resulted in strife and envy among the brethren.

Verse 1: And Jacob dwelt in the land wherein his father was a stranger, in the land of Canaan.

Verse 2: These are the generations of Jacob. Joseph, being seventeen years old, was feeding the flock with his brethren; and the lad was with the sons of Bilhah, and with the sons of Zilpah, his father's wives: and Joseph brought unto his father their evil report.

Verse 3: Now Israel loved Joseph more than all his children, because he was the son of his old age: and he made him a coat of many colours.

The "coat of many colors" is a mistranslation. He made him a long robe with sleeves. The man who labored at every day tasks, wore a seamless robe; we note here that our Lord Jesus wore the cloak of the poor. *"Then the soldiers, when they had crucified Jesus, took his garments, and made four parts, to every soldier a part; and also his coat: now the coat was without seam, woven from the top throughout" (John 19:23).* It was a tailored garment that was worn by those who did not have to work.

The brothers doubtless knew that Reuben would lose the birthright, and when Joseph appeared in this robe, it signified that he was Jacob's heir, and the object of special favors. So they hated him without cause.

Joseph told his aged father the evil things his brothers were doing, so they hated him all the more. It got to the point they could not say a kind word to him. Jesus came into the world and walked among His own, and they would not acknowledge Him.

Jacob sent Joseph from Hebron, where they lived, to Shechem to check on his brothers. When Joseph arrived in Shechem, he found they had moved the flock on up to Dothan, which means Joseph traveled a distance of some 50 miles or more, passing on through the city where the brothers avenged their sister's honor, and burned the town. One might wonder about the "evil reports" that Joseph gave to Israel, but in light of the tender age of Joseph, it could be understood that out of innocency, he reported what the boys talked about around the campfires at night. Such as in chapter 35:22, we read that Israel journeyed and spread his tent beyond the Tower of Eder after Rachel's death, and at that place Reuben slept with Bilhah, and Joseph told Israel about it.

His intentions were certainly honorable. He saw that his brothers were treacherous, murderous, and incestuous. Joseph hated the evil of their ways, and this truth is confirmed, when he refused the advances of his master's wife, when he was sent down into Egypt.

There was something else about young Joseph that the boys hated. He was a dreamer; but his dreams were given to him by God. That was even worse, because it produced spiritual jealousy! Every time he had a good dream, he would run across the fields to share it with his brothers, and that proved to be his downfall. Some things that God gives to His children are not to be shared right on the spot. In the book of Deuteronomy 29:29, we are told, *"The secret things belong unto the Lord our God: but those things which are revealed belong unto us and to our children forever, that we may do all the words of this law."*

"Let me tell you my dream!" he exclaimed innocently:

Verse 7: For, behold, we were binding sheaves in the field, and, lo, my sheaf arose, and also stood upright; and behold, your sheaves stood round about, and made obeisance to my sheaf.

Verse 8: And his brethren said to him, shalt thou indeed reign over us? or shalt though indeed have dominion over us? And they hated him yet the more for his dreams, and for his words.

The answer their brothers gave was proof enough that they recognized that Joseph was chosen of God for a special purpose. *"Just what we thought! You think you are going to be a king over us! Not fair! You are next to the youngest son of our old man, and we resent your implications!"*

A sheaf is the rendering of three Hebrew words: (1) bundle of grain *"alummah,"* bound, (2) bunch *"amir,"* handful, (3) A heap, *"omer."* Under the Mosaic law, the day after the Feast of the Passover, the Hebrews brought into the temple a sheaf of barley, with accompaning ceremonies (Leviticus 23:10-12).

To add hurt to their injury, Joseph had yet another dream, and he not only told his brother about the dream, but he excitedly shared it with his father. He dreamed that the sun, the moon, and the eleven stars bowed down to him.

155

Verse 9: And he dreamed yet another dream, and told it his brethren, and said, Behold, I have dreamed a dream more; and, behold, the sun and the moon and the eleven stars made obeisance to me.

Verse 10: And he told it to his father, and to his brethren: and his father rebuked him, and said unto him, What is this dream that thou hast dreamed? Shall I and thy mother and thy brethren indeed come to bow down ourselves to thee to the earth?

Verse 11: And his brethren envied him: but his father observed the say.

In Luke 2:19, we read how Mary pondered these things in her heart. *"But Mary kept all these things, and pondered them in her heart."* Thus it happened that when Jacob sent Joseph to Shechem to see about the brothers, they plotted his death when they saw him coming.

Verse 19: And they said one to another, Behold, this dreamer cometh.

Verse 20: Come now therefore, and let us slay him, and cast him into some pit, and we will say, Some evil beast hath devoured him: and we shalls ee what will become of his dreams.

Verse 21: And Reuben heard it, and he delivered him out of their hands; and said, Let us not kill him.

Verse 22: And Reuben said unto them, Shed no blood, but cast him into this pit that is in the wilderness, and lay no hand upon him; that he might rid him out of their hands, to deliver him to his father again.

Reuben had full intentions of rescuing Joseph from the pit as soon as the brothers were gone. They took young Joseph and cast him to the empty pit, and while they were eating their lunch not far from the well, they spied a company of Ishmaelites from Gilead traveling towards Egypt to sell their spices of balm and myrrh. *"And when they were come into the house, they saw the young child with Mary his mother, and fell down, and worshipped him: and when they had opened their treasures, and myrrh" (Matthew 2:11).* In Jeremiah 8:22, we read the cry, *"Is there no balm in Gilead; is there no physician there . . .?"*

They sold Joseph that day to the Arabs for 20 pieces of silver, while Joseph was begging for mercy. It did not take long for those cries to reach the ears of his brothers, but it took over twenty years for repentance to come to their hardened hearts. In 42:21, we are told, *"And they said one to another, We are guilty concerning our brother, in that we saw the anguish of his soul, when he besought us, and we would not hear; therefore is this distress come upon us."*

The envy of the brothers led to violence and anger. With hearts full of malice and hatred, they sold their brother into slavery, and added to their crime, a lie to cover up their murderous intent. They killed an innocent animal (goat) and splattered its blood all over the coat of many colors, and took it home to Jacob vowing they found the coat, but Joseph was no where around.

One might have had a flash of appreciation for Reuben, for had he not intended to come back to the well and rescue his little brother? Had he not cried in anguish and rent his clothes when he discovered Joseph was gone —sold to the Midianites; yet he stood silently by and became a party to their lies to Jacob; if we are to understand fully that Reuben knew the truth at that time. He was away from the camp when they traded Joseph for money.

22. JOSEPH FOUND FAVOR
(Genesis 39-41)

When Jacob heard the news about Joseph, he was so full of grief that he tore his clothes and put sackcloth (rough clothes) on his loins and cried, *"I will go down to my grave mourning his death. I shall never be consoled by any of you."* A period of 22 years would go by before he would really know the truth.

We will only briefly mention chapter 38 and the sins of Judah. We might wonder why this story is inserted between the time Joseph was sold, and his arrival down in Egypt. It is not a very pleasant story, but we realize it has significance and spiritual purpose.

The Lord was against his children marrying into the godless line of Canaanites. He would show us by this episode in the life of Judah that His election stands sure, and He will develop for Himself a people. Judah made no attempt to rise above the deceitful and lustful ways of his brothers. He sowed his seed of mischief and betrayal, and reaped the whirlwind through his own sons and daughters. The most important fact about this story is that the baby born of Judah's unholy act, became an ancestor of our Lord Jesus Christ. In Hebrews 7:14 we read, *"For it is evident that our Lord sprang out of Judah."* Our Lord and Saviour who took on the form of man, chose a lineage that included Gentile women, who were under a curse (Tamar, Rahab, Ruth, Bathsheba), and men no more righteous than the women. This woman Tamar had the privilege of being one of the few women whose names are listed in the genealogy of Jesus our Lord.

Now, our story continues to chapter 39 with Joseph being sold for the second time. Soon after his arrival in Egypt, the Ishmaelite traders sold him to Potiphar, a member of the personal staff of Pharaoh, king of Egypt. Potiphar noted that everything Joseph did succeeded.

Verse 2: And the Lord was with Joseph, and he was a prosperous man; and he was in the house of his master the Egyptian.

Verse 4: And Joseph found grace in his sight, and he served him: and he made him overseer over his house, and all that he had he put into his hand.

Verse 5: And it came to pass from the time that he had made him overseer in his house, and over all that he had, that the Lord blessed the Egyptian's house for Joseph's sake; and the blessing of the Lord was upon all that he had in the house, and in the field.

Verse 6: And he left all that he had in Joseph's hand; and he knew not ought he had, save the bread which he did eat. And Joseph was a goodly person, and well favoured.

Potiphar had at last found a man who could manage his entire estate with absolute efficiency; and one who would not steal him blind. He knew that Joseph's God was blessing him in a way that his many gods had never done. But Joseph's prosperity stirred up the nest of Satan.

Potiphar's wife took hold of Joseph and tried to seduce him. He politely refused her advances with these words: *"I cannot do this great wickedness, and sin against God."* She did not give up. This must have tried young Joseph sorely for we are told she plagued him day by day; then she "set her trap." She found Joseph in the house alone and she grabbed at him, but when he fled from her he left his garment. She cried loud and long, *"See, this Hebrew has mocked us. He came into the hosue while my husband was gone and tried to rape me! Here is the proof!"*

The men of the house told their master, and Joseph was bound and thrown into the prison; a place where the king's prisoners were kept.

Verse 21: But the Lord was with Joseph, and showed him mercy, and gave him favour in the sight of the keeper of the prison.

Verse 22: And the keeper of the prison committed to Joseph's hand all the prisoners that were in the prison; and whatsoever they did there, he was the doer of it.

Verse 23: The keeper of the prison looked not to any thing that was under his hand; because the Lord was with him, and that which he did, the Lord made it to prosper.

We should note here that Potiphar was captain of the king's bodyguard, and probably in charge of all administrative duties for Pharaoh. He was called an "officer" of Pharaoh, and the Hebrew word is *"saris"* which means *"eunuch,"* and in the pagan countries quite often they would castrate the men closely associated with the king's court to keep them loyal, or to prevent them from producing their own dynasty. Thus, the possibility exists that Potiphar was a "true" eunuch.

In Psalm 105:17-19, we read this about the sovereignty of God in the life of Joseph, *"He sent a man, before them, even Joseph, who was sold for a servant: Whose feet they hurt with fetters: he was laid in iron: Until the time that his word came: the word of the Lord tried him."*

THE BUTLER AND THE BAKER

The king of Egypt became angry with his butler (wine taster), and his baker, and he threw them into the prison where Joseph took charge of them. The Holy Spirit did not tell us the nature of their offense; but their titles would suggest to us the nature of their crime. We are told they were in the prison for a "season" under his care; the word "season" in Hebrew means a full year went by, then they each had a dream which troubled them.

Their countenance fell and they were bothered deeply about the meaning of their dreams: Joseph said, *". . . Do not interpretations belong to God? Tell me them, I pray you."*

The chief butler told his dream first: he saw before him a vine that had three branches; it was budding, its blossoms shot forth, and the clusters thereof brought forth ripe grapes. And Pharaoh's cup was in his hand. He took the grapes, and he pressed them into Pharaoh's cup, and he gave the cup to his king.

Joseph gave this interpretation: three branches equal three days; within three days the king will restore you to your position in the palace.

Joseph inserted some thoughts of his own at that moment. He asked the butler to remember him to the king when he received his pardon. This is the first time we hear Joseph pleading his case. He told the butler how he had been taken from his family and sold into slavery, and that he was also innocent though in the prison.

When the baker saw that Joseph had given the butler a good interpretation, he quickly told him his dream.

The baker dreamed he had three baskets of white bread on his head. In the top basket he had all kinds of pastries for the Pharoah, but the birds came and ate them.

Joseph gave this interpretation to the baker's dream: the three baskets mean three days; within three days the king will lift your head from your shoulders, and put your body up on a pole, so the birds can feast on your flesh.

Within three days God fulfilled the interpretations that Joseph had given to the baker and the butler. The butler was restored to his position before the king, and the baker was beheaded. But the butler did not remember Joseph at that time.

At the end of two more years in prison, Joseph was called to interpret a dream for the Pharaoh. He was troubled in his spirit about the meaning of his dream. In chapter 41:9, we read, *"Then spake the chief butler unto Pharaoh, saying, I do remember my faults this day"* He suddenly remembered Joseph who had long ago interpreted his dream, but he had failed to mention his name before the king.

It seems more in line with the ways of God to view this delay as the perfect "timing" of God rather than disobedience or distrust on the part of Joseph who had hardly murmured about his lot for the last twelve years. Joseph was seventeen when he was sold into slavery, and he was thirty when he was put in charge of Pharaoh's grain program.

By this dream (and others) we learn that God can use the ungodly when it suits His purpose. Pharaoh dreamed a dream that led to the exhaltation of Joseph. The king dreamed that he was standing by the Nile River, when suddenly seven sleek, fat cows rose up out of the water and began eating the grass. Then seven other cows came up from the river, but these were skinny and their ribs were protruding. They walked over and stood beside the fat cows. The skinny cows ate the fat cows. Then the Pharaoh woke up from the dream.

He went back to sleep and dreamed again: he saw seven heads of grain on one stalk, with every kernel well formed and plump. Suddenly, seven more heads appeared on the stalk, but they were shriveled and withered by the east wind. The thin heads swallowed up the seven plump, well-formed heads. He woke up the second time and realized he had been dreaming.

Verse 14: Then Pharaoh sent and called Joseph, and they brought him hastily out of the dungeon: and he shaved himself, and changed his raiment, and came in unto Pharaoh.

Verse 15: And Pharaoh said unto Joseph, I have dreamed a dream, and there is none that can interpret it: and I have heard say of thee, that thou canst understand a dream to interpret.

Verse 16: And Joseph answered Pharaoh, saying, It is not in me: God shall give Pharaoh an answer of peace.

The Pharaoh related his two dreams to Joseph, and he told him the two dreams were one, for they had the same meaning. Joseph told the king that God was showing him in advance something that was to soon take place. The seven good kine represent seven years; the seven good ears represent seven years; the seven lean and ill-favored kine that came up after them are seven years; and the seven empty ears blasted by the east wind are seven years of famine. It simply means that the land will have seven good years of plenty, and then seven years of severe famine; the double dream was meant to give double impact to the truth and the importance of the situation ahead for Pharaoh.

In the life of Joseph we learn that the way up is down. God has said to us He will exalt us in due time. God was moving to bring His people into the land of Egypt; and Joseph and his brothers would remember the dreams he had at seventeen.

Verse 33: Now therefore let Pharaoh look out a man discreet and wise, and set him over the land of Egypt.

Verse 34: Let Pharaoh do this, and let him appoint officers over the land, and take up the fifth part of the land of Egypt in the seven plenteous years.

Verse 35: And let them gather all the food of those good years that come, and lay up corn under the hand of Pharaoh, and let them keep food in the cities.

Verse 36: And that food shall be for store to the land against the seven years of famine, which shall be in the land of Egypt; that the land perish not through the famine.

Pharaoh liked what he heard; he knew he couldn't find a better man than Joseph to handle his affairs. In verse 38, we read, "... *Can we find such a one as this is, a man in whom the spirit of God is?*"

He put Joseph in charge over his house, to rule the people. He took off his own ring and put it upon Joseph's hand, clothed him in fine linen, and put a gold chain about his neck; he put him in the second chariot, and caused the people of Egypt to bow down to him.

Pharaoh gave Joseph an Egyptian name, "Zaphnath-paaneah" which meant "Saviour of the World." He gave him Asenath for his wife, and they had two children: Manesseh (Forgetting), and Ephraim, (Fruitful).

Joseph traveled over all Egypt gathering up food and storing it in the storehouses in preparation for the days of the famine. In seven years the famine hit, but there was bread in Egypt.

23. THE SONS OF ISRAEL
(Genesis 42-45) (1678 B.C.)

FAMINE IN THE LAND

The famine which had covered the land of Egypt reached out to Canaan and other lands of the region. All of Israel's sons, but Benjamin, traveled to Egypt to buy corn, Jacob said, *". . . Behold, I have heard that there is corn in Egypt."*

Verse 7: And Joseph saw his brethren, and he knew them, but made himself strange unto them, and spake roughly unto them; and he said unto them, Whence come ye? And they said, From the land of Canaan to buy food.

Verse 8: And Joseph knew his brethren, but they knew not him.

Verse 9: And Joseph remembered the dreams which he dreamed of them, and said unto them, Ye are spies; to see the nakedness of the land ye are come.

There would have been no way for these men to know that it was Joseph from whom they would buy the corn. He stood before them, but they did not recognize their own brother. It had been over 20 years since they had sold him into slavery. Now they were hungry, and Joseph had the bread. By his very name, he had become the saviour of the people. In Jeremiah 16:17, we read, *"For My eyes are on all their ways; they are not hidden from My face, nor is their iniquity concealed from My eyes."*

The brothers pleaded with the governor of the land in their own behalf. *"We are 12 brothers, and one is home with our aged father, and one is not."* Joseph still insisted that they were spies, and said the only way they could prove their innocence was to send for their youngest brother *"One of you will go after your youngest brother and the rest will stay here with me bound in the prison house. If you do not have a younger brother, then I will know you are spies."*

Joseph kept them in his prison for three days, then he called them forth. *"I fear God, and love Him with all my heart, so I will give you an opportunity to prove to me whether you are lying or not. Only one of you shall remain in chains in jail, and I will let the rest of you go home with grain for your families. When you return, bring your youngest brother."*

Multiplied words have been written about the reason Joseph so adamantly insisted they were spies; since we know that vengeance belongs to God, we must conclude that he was totally committed to the will of God in the restoration of his family. Joseph surely must have been just as surprised to see his brothers as they were, later, to discover his true identity. He had lived the last 20 years of his adult life among the Egyptians; their habits, ways, and language had become a part of his way of life. The brothers had not changed so drastically. When he put them in the ward, it gave him some time to think about the best way to handle them. He had to have time to seek the face of the Lord.

When Joseph demanded that the youngest be brought to him, the brothers, who had carried a lie in their heart for 20 years, confessed their evil deed among themselves not realizing Joseph knew their language, too.

Verse 21: And they said one to another, We are verily guilty concerning our brother, in that we saw the anguish of his soul, when he besought us, and we would not hear; therefore is this distress come upon us.

Verse 22: And Reuben answered them, saying, Spake I not unto you saying, Do not sin against the child; and ye would not hear? Therefore, behold, also his blood is required.

Verse 23: And they knew not that Joseph understood them; for he spake unto them by an interpreter.

Verse 24: And he turned himself about from them, and wept; and returned to them again, and communed with them, and took from them Simeon, and bound him before their eyes.

Through the actions of Joseph, the Lord was showing the children of Israel their transgressions, and He used it to discipline them. As for Joseph, *"He wept."* In Luke 19:41, we are told that Jesus beheld the city of Jerusalem, and He wept over it.

Then Joseph commanded their vessels to be filled with corn, and all their money be restored to them. He added provisions for their journey back to Jacob. The brothers left for home. In the late of evening when they stopped for the night, one of them opened

170

his sack and found the money. They were all filled with terror. *"What is God doing to us?"* they cried! We will be killed for this! They came to Jacob in the land of Canaan, and they told him their story. One might well imagine this scene. The aged Jacob endeavored to put the story together while nine sons were excitedly talking all at once. How many times did they relive their experiences of the past few weeks, as they traveled towards their own homeland rehearsing over and over what they could tell their father? Their sins had found them out. Could he live through the ordeal? Would he allow Benjamin to go into Egypt?

Verse 35: And it came to pass as they emptied their sacks, that, behold, every man's bundle of money was in his sack: and when both they and their father saw the bundles of money, they were afraid.

Jacob was beside himself with grief. *"You have taken away my children-Joseph never came back, Simeon is now gone, and you want to take Benjamin into a strange land! No! No! He cannot go!"* Jacob, believing those 20 years that Joseph was dead, remembered that with Benjamin gone, he would have nothing left of his sons by his beloved Rachel.

In chapter 42:37, it was Reuben who tried to persuade Jacob to let them take Benjamin back to Egypt. He offered his own two sons as surety of Benjamin's safe return. This offer seemed a little hollow and empty considering the fact that he knew the truth about the coat of many colors, and he never said a word all those years.

In chapter 43:2, Judah stepped forth as the spokesman for the brethren. He reminded Jacob that they were out of corn, and they could not show their face again in Egypt without the youngest brother. *"We cannot go without him, for we will all be killed by the governor of the land! The man asked us of our family. He wanted to know if you were well, and he asked if we had yet another brother."*

Verse 8: And Judah said unto Israel his father, Send the lad with me, and we will arise and go; that we may live, and not die, both we, and thou, and also our little ones.

Verse 9: I will be surety for him; of my hand shalt thou require him: if I bring him not unto thee, and set him before thee, then let me bear the blame forever:

Jacob agreed to send Benjamin to Egypt lest they all die in the land of Canaan from starvation; he sent gifts to be presented to *"the man" down in Egypt. "Take double your money, and take with you the money you brought home with you."*

Verse 14: And God Almighty give you mercy before the man, that he may send away your brother, and Benjamin. If I be bereaved of my children, I am bereaved.

COME AND DINE

When the brothers arrived in Egypt they went immediately to stand before Joseph with their brother Benjamin. Joseph held his emotions though his hungry eyes had at last beheld his little brother. He ordered his servants to prepare a feast and bring the men to his personal home. *"They will dine with me."*

Still the brothers were afraid. They questioned Joseph's household manager; we are not told about the language they used, but the man assured the brothers that he had received money for the grain they carried with them.

Verse 23: And he said, Peace be to you, fear not: your God, and the God of your father, hath given you treasure in your sacks; I had your money, And he brought Simeon out unto them.

Joseph's man gave the brothers water to wash their feet, and food for their animals. They got their presents ready to present to Joseph when he came home. *"When Joseph came home, they presented him with their gifts, and bowed low before him"*

Joseph asked, *"Is your father well. Is he yet alive?"*

They answered, *"He is yet alive; and they bowed down and gave obeisance."*

Joseph lifted up his eyes and saw again his brother Benjamin, his mother's son, and said, *"Is this your younger brother, of whom ye spake unto me? And he said, "God be gracious unto thee, my son."*

Joseph was hurting inside, so he sought the privacy of his own chamber, and there he wept; he washed his face and returned to the dining room, and said *"Set on the bread."*

Joseph ate by himself. His brothers were served at a separate table, and the Egyptians at still another table, because the Egyptians hated the Hebrews, and it was an abomination for them to eat at the same table with them. Joseph gave the seating places for each of his brothers. He seated them in the order of their ages, from the oldest to the youngest, much to their amazement, and their food was served from his own table. He gave an extra large plate of food for Benjamin, and they wined and dined that night with the man who was second to the king of Egypt.

JUDAH PLEADS FOR BENJAMIN

In chapter 44, the brothers prepared to leave; Joseph ordered his household manager to fill each of their sacks with all the grain they could carry, and to return to each man his money. *"Put my silver cup at the top of Benjamin's sack, along with the grain money."* They were hardly out of sight, when Joseph told his manager, *"Follow them, and ask them why they are rewarding my favors to them with evil?"*

The man did as he was commanded and overtook the brothers, and said *"Why have you stolen my lord's silver drinking cup, which he uses for fortune-telling when he was so good to you. Do you repay good for evil?"*

Verse 7: And they said unto him, Wherefore saith my lord these words? God forbid that thy servants should do according to this thing:

Verse 8: Behold, the money, which we found in our sacks' mouth, we brought again unto thee out of the land of Canaan: how then should we steal out of thy lord's house silver or gold?

Verse 9: With whomsoever of thy servants it be found, both let him die, and we also will be my lord's bondman.

The man said only the man who stole the cup would be a slave; the rest could go free. They searched the sacks and found the cup in Benjamin's bag. The brothers literally ripped their clothing in despair; they were commanded to return to the city to face Joseph and confess to their crime.

Joseph was slowly pulling a confession out of his brothers. It would be easier on them if they could have made it this time. The lie could still go undetected. When they reached Joseph's house, the men fell on their faces before him to plead their innocence.

Judah began to plead the desperate prayer of the lost ". . . *What shall we say unto my Lord? what shall we speak? or how shall we clear ourselves? God hath found out the iniquity of thy servants: behold, we are my lord's servants, both we, and he also with whom the cup is found.*"

Judah was really saying, "We are sunk! No use going home to our aged dad now for without Benjamin, he will die. We took Joseph from him, and now this will finish him off. No. We will all stay right here and be this man's slaves." Judah was admitting that all the brothers had come to the end of themselves. No amount of pleading could help them now.

Verse 17: And he said, God forbid that I should do so: but the man in whose hand the cup is found, he shall be my servant; and as for you, get you up in peace unto your father.

Peace! Again Judah stepped forth to plead their case. *"How can we plead, my lord? What can we say to change your mind? Please be patient with me, and hear me out, though I know you are next to the Pharaoh himself, and could doom me on the spot. I cannot go back home without the lad."*

Judah recounted the entire story of how Joseph had asked about the brothers, and the old father, and if we were still alive, and how he had rather be dead than return to Jacob without Benjamin.

Verse 30: Now therefore when I come to thy servant my father, and the lad be not with us; seeing that his life is bound up in the lad's life.;

Verse 31: It shall come to pass, when he seeth that the lad is not with us, that he will die: and thy servants, shall bring down the gray hairs of thy servant our father with sorrow to the grave.

Verse 32: For they servant became surety for the lad unto my father, saying, If I bring him not unto thee, then I shall bear the blame to my father forever.

In this story seven times it stated that *"Joseph wept."* In chapter 45:1, we are told that he could not longer contain himself. He ordered all the servants to leave the room, and there alone with his 11 brothers, he made himself known to them.

Verse 2: And he wept aloud: and the Egyptians and the house of Pharaoh heard.

Verse 3: And Joseph said unto his brethren, I am Joseph; doth my father yet live? and his brethren could not answer him; for they were troubled at his presence.

Verse 4: And Joseph said unto his brethren, Come near to me I pray you. And they came near. And he said, I am Joseph your brother, whom ye sold in Egypt.

In Luke 24:39, we compare, *"Behold, My hands and my feet, that it is I, myself; handle me and see."* In John 14:9, *"Have I been so long time with you, and yet hast thou not known me?"* *"Let not your hearts be troubled . . ." (John 14:1).*

This had to be Joseph for no one else would have known that story. It is doubtful that Benjamin ever knew what they had done to his brother. This was probably the first time he heard of their treachery.

Verse 5: Now therefore be not grieved, nor angry with yourselves, that ye sold me hither: for God did send me before you to preserve life.

Verse 6: For these two years hath the famine been in the land: and yet there are five years, in the which there shall neither be earing nor harvest.

Verse 7: And God sent me before you to preserve you a posterity in the earth, and to save your lives by a great deliverance.

Verse 8: So now it was not you that sent me hither, but God: and he hath made me a father to Pharaoh, and lord of all his house, and a ruler throughout all the land of Egypt.

No longer speaking through an interpreter, he announced in their own language, *"I am Joseph!"* Then quickly helping them to recover from the shock by speaking to them a prophecy. He had indeed been sent to deliver them. Had this particular incident not happened in their history, the children of Israel would have lived in Canaan and intermarried with the Ishmaelites, Edomites, and the Canannites, and scattered all over the land. They were called to be a peculiar people; a people separated unto God simply because He loved them, and not because of any good thing that they could accomplish on their own. *"For thou art an holy people unto the Lord thy God: the Lord thy God hath chosen thee to be a special people unto himself, above all people that are upon the face of the earth. The Lord did not set his love upon you, nor choose you, because ye were more in number than any people; for ye were the fewest of all people: But because he would keep the oath which he had sworn unto your fathers, hath the Lord brought you out with a mighty hand, and redeemed you out of the house of bondmen from the hand of Pharaoh king of Egypt"* *(Deuteronomy 7:6-8).*

Joseph urged them to hurry back home and tell their father that he was well down in Egypt. *"Bring him here to me, and you will live in the land of Goshen, and you will never again want for food or anything for I am second to the king in this land."* Then he fell on Benjamin's neck, and they wept on each others shoulders.

When the news spread to the Pharoah that Joseph's brothers were with him out of Canaan, he sent word for them to return and bring their father to Egypt, and he would assign them the very best of territory. In verse 20, he said, *"Also regard not your stuff; for the good of all the land of Egypt is yours."*

It would be difficult to imagine a more touching scene than this we have just covered, unless it would be Israel when he looked out across the field and saw his sons coming home. When he saw the wagons pulling in at his door, his heart surely began to skip and beat rapidly. He heard them shouting—again they were all talking at one time, *"Joseph is alive! Yes, he is alive!"* But Israel did not believe them at first. He was too old, and the years had been too full of misery for him to grasp the meaning of all the joy. They settled down and told the whole story.

Verse 28: And Israel said, It is enough, Joseph my son is yet alive: I will go and see him before I die.

24. ISRAEL IN EGYPT
(Genesis 46-50) (1677 B.C.)

With our journey through Genesis almost ended, we must keep in mind that the primary reason God delivered the children of Israel into the hands of the Egyptians was to develop a pure Jewish line; it was an abomination to their God for them to marry outside their own heritage. When the Jewish people of today see Jesus as their Messiah, they will rejoice in the fact that there is no bondage in Him. He came to liberate them. Now, Jew and Gentile alike are all "one" in the Lord Jesus.

In chapter 46, one cannot help but revel in the good news that Israel is going to Egypt to see his long lost son. After the birth of Jesus, God spoke to Joseph and told him to take the baby and journey into Egypt for Herod was killing all the male children from birth to two years old. In Matthew 2:1-13-15, we read, *"And when they were departed, behold, the angel of the Lord appeareth to Joseph in a dream, saying, Arise, and take the young child and his mother, and flee into Egypt, and be thou there until I bring thee word: for Herod will seek the young child to destroy him. When he arose, he took the young child and his mother by night, and departed into Egypt: and was there until the death of Herod: that it might be fulfilled which was spoken of the Lord by the prophet, saying, Out of Egypt have I called my son."*

Verse 1: And Israel took his journey with all that he had, and came to Beer-sheba, and offered sacrifices unto the God of his father Isaac.

Verse 2: And God spake unto Israel in the visions of the night, and said, Jacob, Jacob, And he said, Here am I.

Verse 3: And he said, I am God, the God of thy father: fear not to go down into Egypt; for I will there make of thee a great nation:

Verse 4: I will go down with thee into Egypt; and I will also surely bring thee up again: and Joseph shall put his hand upon thine eyes.

Israel knew from his father that God had promised them the land of Canaan. He was old by now; yet he knew he had to pull up stakes and go into Egypt for his son was yet alive. He had to see Joseph before he died. If he ever needed encouragement about a decision, it was now. He traveled along with mixed emotions about this strange land. He was actually leaving the home of his father, Abraham, and with all the promises that had been handed down to them yet to be realized. But without Joseph, what could it mean anyway? He was his son by the wife of his youth, and he had loved her enough to give 14 years of hard work to Laban, her father, to wed her. She was his favorite, and so was Joseph. By the time he reached Beer-sheba, he knew it was time to offer up the sacrifice of repentance unto the God of his fathers.

It was there that God spoke to him in a night vision. The help had at last come. The voice of "Elohim" reached him during the night. He called Jacob by his old name. Each time he had made an important move, God had spoken to him directly.

When he left his parents to go to Haran, God had appeared to him at Bethel. (28:13-15); when he had instructed him to go back to Canaan, (31:3); when he left Shechem, God appeared to him, (35:1, 9-12). Thus, it was time to offer sacrifices and hear from the Lord.

(1) I am God (I AM)
(2) The God of your father
(3) Fear not
(4) I will make of thee a great nation
(5) I will go down with thee
(6) I will also surely bring you out
(7) Joseph will bury you

We must remember that Beersheba was near the southern boundary of the land, and Israel was crossing over to the *"place of no return."* The words, *"I will surely bring you out,"* was a prediction that would not be fulfilled until after Jacob's death. It would, of course, be 400 plus years before God, by the hand of Moses, delivered them from the hand of a Pharoah who knew not Joseph.

Jacob rose up from Beersheba, and was carried by the sons of Israel, with all the wives and little ones, in wagons that had been furnished by the king of Egypt. Wagon by wagon, mile after mile, the twelve sons of Israel (the foundation of Israel), walked and rode till they entered the land of Goshen, the place where grazing was at its best. God plans His best for those He loves. The Lord never takes us part of the way in life to leave us. Man left to his own devices will "self-destruct." Faith will always bridge the gap between what we see, and what God has promised will come to pass. In the land of Goshen, God would develop a nation of peculiar people called unto Himself. His Word stand sure; what He has spoken will come to pass.

Seventy souls went down into Egypt. That does not include, of course, the servants, or the daughters-in-law, who are not considered "his seed." Remember three souls were already in Egypt: Joseph, Manasseh, and Ephraim. The number seventy became associated with the nation Israel after that in several particular ways. In Numbers 11:16 — seventy elders; II Chronicles 36:21, seventy years of captivity; Daniel 9:24 seventy weeks determined on the people for their transgressions; Luke 10:1, Jesus sent out the seventy witnesses, two by two; it is believed that seventy men made up the Sanhedrin in the days of Christ.

Jacob sent Judah ahead of the train to tell Joseph that they were almost there, and would soon be arriving in Goshen. Joseph lost no time ordering his chariot ready; he hastened to the side of his father, and they fell into each others arms without a word. They sobbed and cried unable to speak at first. The sons of Israel wept as their aged father was united with the son of Rachel, his beloved wife. Finally, after their tears of joy turned into laughter of relief, Jacob held Joseph at arm's length, looked into his face and said, *"Let me now die, for I have seen your face again."*

In the days of Moses, each plague God brought upon the Egyptians represented one of their gods. They had no knowledge of the true God, and had changed *"the glory of the incorruptible God into an image made like to corruptible man, and to birds, and fourfooted beasts, and creeping things" (Romans 1:23).*

In India the men who skin cows for leather (chamar chaste) are outcasts. The Word of God teaches that men are to have dominion over cattle, but in Egypt the cattle had dominion over men.

God would be praised in all He performs. He sent them to a land where even their occupation was a stench to the inhabitants. Each step we take must be ordered by God; He will receive the glory for our deliverance. The man who takes even an ounce of credit for having ordered his life is a man who does not know the God of Abraham, Isaac, and Jacob. Jesus Himself said He could do nothing without listening to hear from the Father. Is that not our example even these thousands of years later?

Joseph announced his family to Pharaoh, taking five of his brothers with him to stand in the presence of the king. The first question that popped out of the mouth of the king was *"What is your occupation?"*

Joseph had briefed them as to what they should say. In chapter 47:4, we read, *"They said, moreover unto Pharaoh, For to sojourn in the land are we come; for thy servants have no pasture for their flocks; for the famine is sore in the land of Canaan: now therefore, we pray thee, let thy servants dwell in the land of Goshen."*

Joseph proved that day that he still had a pure heart undefiled by the ways of the world; he stood before the very king and ruler of the land with his *"shepherd"* family speaking in their behalf, and perhaps even as the interpreter. These crude Canaanites were his very own flesh and blood, and he was not too proud to claim kinship. How he loved them!

Too often in our day and age, men and women who attain to the highest places fail to remember the *"lesser"* ones who helped them succeed. Often when a man looks down from the top of the ladder, he sees only his own footprints.

Pharaoh turned to Joseph and spoke saying, *"Your family, has come to stay with you; the land of Egypt is before you. Choose the best part of the land for them to settle in. That would be the land of Goshen, since they are shepherds. Put some of your brothers who are most capable over my own cattle."* And Jacob blessed Pharaoh.

The Pharaoh turned then to Jacob and asked him his age. The Holy Spirit had a special reason for that type of question to come from a monarch who obviously had very little in common with Jacob and his sons. In verse 7 we are told that Jacob blessed the Pharaoh. We are required to be spiritually alert when reading such passages. The king no doubt felt he was talking to a man of great wisdom and spiritual depth.

Verse 9: And Jacob said unto Pharaoh, The years of my pilgrimage are an hundred and thirty years: few and evil have the days of the years of my life been, and have not attained unto the days of the years of the life of my fathers in the days of their pilgrimage.

Verse 10: And Jacob blessed Pharaoh, and went out from before Pharaoh.

Verse 11: And Joseph placed his father and his brethren, and gave them a possession in the land of Egypt, in the Rameses, as Pharaoh had commanded.

Verse 12: And Joseph nourished his father, and his brethren, and all his father's household, with bread, according to their families.

At a time when there was no bread in the land, Joseph had bread for his family. From the book of Genesis (beginnings), to the book of Revelation (endings), God has proclaimed that the righteous will prosper in famine. Abraham prospered in the land of Egypt during famine; Isaac sowed in the land and God prospered him during famine. In Psalm 37:19, we read, *"The days of the righteous are known to the Lord, and their prosperity will endure forever. In time of disaster they will be sustained; in the days of famine, they will enjoy plenty."*

The weeks of famine continued with no relief in sight. Both the land of Egypt and the land of Canaan were languishing from the lack of food. The only way we can imagine how much grain Joseph stored up during those good years, is to view it in light of the desperate need of the people during the seven years of famine; and he had bread for the land. The people began to come to him to buy from his storehouse.

Joseph brought the money he collected from the people into the house of Pharaoh; and when the money was gone in both lands, Joseph heard their cries for more food for their little ones.

"Our money is gone, but we are starving. Please give us bread, 'Zaphenath-paneah,' or we will die right here before your eyes!" Joseph was not at liberty to give away that which did not really belong to him. He had been selected by the Pharaoh as second in command when he first came to the attention of the king because of his business ability. He told the people to bring their cattle and herds and he would give them bread in exchange. Soon all their livestock and their money was in the hands of the Pharaoh. Unless we understand that famine is a type of judgment over sin, we might be a little critical of Joseph and his methods. We are here dealing with a godless nation. In the land of Canaan, as already pointed out, idolatry was the religion. However, nestled in a *"God-appointed"* corner of the earth, was the *"apple of His eye,"* well-fed and rapidly multiplying. The wisdom of God was operating in Joseph. (It seems apparent that the people were not willing to kill their cattle; perhaps this had to do with their idolatrous belief that cattle were sacred.)

One year they traded for their money; one year they traded for their cattle and herds; the next year they were back, and all they had left to trade was their land and their working hands. They offered themselves to the Pharaoh for food. They needed seed, also, so the land would not lay desolate.

The land of Egypt fell into the hands of the Pharaoh; and the only land he did not buy was the land belonging to the priests; their allotment came from the Pharaoh himself, and they did not have to buy and trade to stay alive. Joseph then scattered the people all over the borders of Egypt, and put them to work. He gave them grain with which to sow the field, and when they harvested, one-fifth of it would belong to the king. He exacted a tax of 20 percent from the people to be paid when the crops were gathered in at the end of each year. He provided the seed, and gave them land to work, and in turn they would return a portion to Pharaoh.

Jacob lived in the land of Egypt for seventeen years; at the age of 147 the time drew near for him to die, so he called his family in to receive their inheritance.

Verse 29: And the time drew nigh that Israel must die: and he called his son Joseph, and said unto him, If now I have found grace in thy sight, put, I pray thee, thy hand under my thigh, and deal kindly and truly with me; bury me not, I pray thee, in Egypt.

Verse 30: But I will lie with my fathers, and thou shalt carry me out of Egypt, and bury me in their burying place. And he said, I will do as thou hast said.

Verse 31: And he said, Swear unto me. And he sware unto him. And Israel bowed himself upon the bed's head.

In gratitude for all that God had let his eyes behold, Israel bowed his head and worshipped God. He must have poured out his heart to the Lord in hopeful anticipation of soon joining his grandfather Abraham, and his father Isaac, and his beloved wife Rachel.

Joseph was a very busy man, so he returned to his work; soon he got the news that his aged father was dying. He took his two sons born to him in Egypt and went to Jacob's bedside. When Joseph arrived, Jacob revived and sat up in bed, and began to rehearse the story of their salvation. *"The El Shaddai appeared to me at Luz in the land of Canaan and blessed me, and promised to make of me a great nation; He gave unto us all the land of Canaan, to us and to our offspring after us. It is our everlasting possession. Bring forth your two sons, Ephraim and Manasseh, for I have a blessing with which to bless them. They will inherit from me also. If you have other sons, they will inherit from you the portion allotted for these two grandsons of mine. Your mother, my beloved Rachel, died after having only two sons, as I traveled from Paddan-aram, only a short distance from Ephrath, and I buried her beside the road going on in to Bethlem."*

Though Joseph was old enough at the time of the death of his mother to remember her, he had been away from home most of his life, and at this point, Israel wanted to renew the story so that Joseph in turn could tell his children about their grandmother.

Jacob looked at the two boys, and said, *"Bring them here, so I can bless them."* He was almost blind from age, so Joseph moved them closer to the old Patriarch. He kissed them and embraced them tenderly, and said *"Joseph, I never thought I would see you alive; now God has not only restored you to me, but he has blessed me by letting me see your children."*

Joseph took the boys by the hand, bowed before his father, and led the them to their grandfather's knees so he could reach them. Joseph put Ephraim at Israel's left hand and Manasseh at his right hand. But Israel crossed his arms, as he stretched them out to lay his hands upon the heads of his two grandsons. He may have been half-blind, but he was still listening to the voice of God who had surely directed him in this blessing. Then he blessed Joseph and his sons. Israel adopted these two sons to represent half a tribe each of Israel; Joseph's name does not appear as one of the twelve tribes. Eventually the name of Reuben would disappear entirely, and the tribe of Simeon would be absorbed in the tribe of Benjamin and Judah. But Ephraim and Manasseh would remain. We are to remember that Reuben sinned against the Lord when he went to bed with his father's wife. Simeon sinned a great sin, when he slaughtered the people at Shechem. To place a child upon the knee was a pledge of adoption. (Still honored among the Orthodox Jews.)

With these words Jacob blessed them, *"May God, the God of my fathers Abraham and Isaac, the God who has shepherded me (fed me), all my life, the Angel who kept me from all evil, bless these lads; and may they bring honor to my name, and to the name of Abraham and Isaac, and may they multiply and become a great nation."*

Joseph apparently had been kneeling with his head bowed and possibly his eyes closed; suddenly, he realized that his father had his right hand upon the head of Ephraim (youngest). He tried to remove Jacob's hand and place it upon the head of Manasseh, (firstborn).

"Not so, my father! Manasseh is my first born!"

Israel refused to change what he had done. *"I know what I am doing my son. Manasseh will become a great people, and he will be great; but his younger brother shall be greater than he, and his seed shall become a multitude of nations. By these two all Israel shall bless each other and say, 'may you be as prosperous as Ephraim and Manasseh.' "*

It is interesting to watch an Orthodox Jewish father on the sabbath evening place his hand on the head of his son and bless him in the very same words that the Holy Spirit spoke through Israel that day so long ago.

Israel said, *"Behold I die: but God shall be with you, and bring you again into the land of your fathers. I have given to you the choice land of Shekem instead of your brothers. I took it from the Amorites with my sword and with my bow."*

In chapter 49, Jacob called in all his sons and said, *"Gather around me for I am dying, and I want to tell you what is going to happen to you in the future.* I will speak to you what God spoke to me. When a man is dying every word takes on special meaning. In verse 2, we are assured that each word he spoke was whispered to Jacob by the Holy Spirit; for is it not highly significant that he used both his names at that particular time?

To Reuben: *"You are my first born, the child of my vigorous youth. You are the head of the list in rank; but you are unstable as water and have forfeited your right as head of the tribe, because you went to the bed of Belhah, and dishonored my name. You have no strength of character so I am demoting you, and you will no longer be first in line."*

It has been written that Reuben's descendants in Jewish history remained true to their ancestral type, unstable as water. They are not often mentioned in Jewish history.

To Simeon and Levi: *"You are two of a kind. Both of you used the weapons of violence against a man, and maimed oxen just for fun. They will live by their instruments of cruelty, Let not my soul come near them. May I never be a party to their wicked plans. I will scatter their descendants throughout Israel."*

The Holy Spirit was reminding them that God had not forgotten how they slaughtered an entire city, and raped the women; while the men could not defend their homes, profaned the Lord's everlasting covenant of circumcision, using it to cripple an entire city.

Judah: *Your brothers shall praise you. You shall destroy your enemies. Your father's sons shall bow before you. Judah, you are a young lion that has finished eating its prey. He has settled down as a lion-who would even dare to approach him? The scepter shall not depart from Judah until Shiloh comes, whom all people shall obey. He has chained his steed to the choicest vine, and washed his clothes in wine. His vesture in the blood of grapes. His eyes shall be red with wine, and his teeth white with milk."*

We are reading a phrophecy of the coming of our Lord and Saviour. The Judah tribe was to be strong and courageous, and their land productive and fruitful. Thus, this tribe would receive the praise of his brethren because the Messiah would come from him. He was the *"meek and lowly"* One in His first coming, but He will return as the *"Lion of the tribe of Judah"* (Revelation 5:5). *"He shall not strive nor cry . . . a bruised reed he shall not break till he send judgment forth to victory" (Matthew 12:19-20).* The scepter (Hebrew *shebet*), is the symbol of rulership. *"Power belongs to God" (Psalm 62:11). "All power is given unto me," (Matthew 28:18). Shiloh has reference to the* Messiah. Wine is the emblem of joy: *"For such joy He endured the cross . . . " (Hebrews 12:2).* He will *"tread the winepress of the fierceness of the wrath of God,"* (Isaiah 63:3; Revelation 14:19-20); then, *"He will come forth with the shout of the merrymaker."* This contrast can only be understood by those who have been washed in the blood of the Lamb.

To Zebulon: *"You shall dwell on the shores of the sea and shall be a harbor for ships, with your borders extending to Sidon."*

Zebulon was to live by the sea and provide a haven for ships. One writer said the Jews were never particularly enamoured of seafaring life, but this reference to Zebulon clearly shows the possibility of this method of living, if they had been willing to seize upon it.

To Issacar: *"You are like a strong ass that comes to rest between sheepfolds. You found a good resting place, the land was good, so you bowed as a servant under his taskmaster."*

NOTES

To Dan: *"You shall judge your people as one of the tribes of Israel. You shall be a serpent in the path that bites the horses' heels, so that the rider falls off."*

This tribe produced only one judge, Sampson, but he was a great man. Sampson, like the serpent, killed the enemy touching him, so that when the horse fell, the rider was brought down with him. Although this tribe produced Sampson, they set up graven images and chose men of the tribe to be priests. In Amos 8:14, we read, *"...god of Dan..."* a term used for devilish idolatry.

Verse 18: I have waited for thy salvation, O Lord.

While blessing his sons, Jacob suddenly relaxed a moment and praised God, and declared that he trusted the salvation and wisdom of God where Dan was concerned. He was prophesying by the Holy Spirit, and some of the things he said, he heard them for the first time. Dan would need to be protected against the things to come. Dan is not mentioned in the book of Revelation.

To Gad: *"A troop shall overcome you; but you shall overcome in the end."*

The sons of Gad were among the most outstanding of the mighty men of David. They were referred to as the mighty men of valor ... In I Chronicles 12:8, 14, we read, *"And the Gadites there separated themselves unto David into the hold to the wilderness men of might, and men of war fit for the battle, that could handle shield and buckler, whose faces were like the faces of lions, and were as swift as the roes upon the mountains;"* One of the judges of Israel, Japthah, came from the tribe of Gad.

To Asher: *"You shall produce foods that shall be fit for kings."*

One translation reads, *"Asher's food shall be rich, and he shall yield royal dainties."* Moses in his farewell song, *"Let Asher be blessed with children, let him be acceptable to his brethren, and let him dip his foot in oil" (Deuteronomy 33:24).*

To Naphtali: *"You shall be like a leaping deer, free running on the hills."*

The most widely known of his descendants is Barak, who, with Deborah, won a mighty victory over Jabin and Sisera of the Canaanites (Judges 4:10, 5:18).

To Joseph: *"You are a fruitful bough; like a fruitful tree beside a fountain, and its branches run over the wall, your enemies hated you without a cause; they shot at you, and hated you; but your bow remained strong, and you were strengthened and your enemies scattered by the Mighty God of Jacob: the Shepherd, the Rock of Israel. Even by the God of your father, so, who shall help you; and by the Almighty, who shall bless you with the blessings of heaven above, blessings of the deep that lieth under, blessings of the breasts, and of the womb: The blessings of your father are mighty beyond the blessing of my progenitors, unto the utmost bound of the everlasting hills. These many blessings shall be on the head of Joseph, and on the crown of the head of him that was separated from his brothers."*

Joseph is said to be *"fruitful."* He became two tribes, and became twice as prosperous as any of his brothers. He typifies our Lord who was the *"beautiful and glorius branch,"* (Isaiah 4:2); whose fruit will someday fill the whole earth (Isaiah 27:6); fruit that will shake like the woods of Lebanon and be as plentiful as grass (Psalm 72:16), as numerous as the stars of heaven (Psalm 15:5), and the sands upon the seashore (Psalm 22:17). In John 15:5, we read, *"I am the vine, ye are the branches: He that abideth in me, and I in him, the same bringeth forth much fruit: for without me ye can do nothing."*

To Benjamin: *"You shall be as the wolf that prowls. You shall devour the enemy in the morning time, and divide the spoil at night."*

The apostle Paul was from the tribe of Benjamin. This smallest of the tribes was ever ready to take up the sword for the honor of the Lord. He would stalk his prey and come back victorious. He would fight while he was young, and divide his spoil in his latter years. In Psalm 68:24-27, we get a true picture of this: *"Thy solemn processions are seen, O God, the processions of my God, my King, into the sanctuary — the singers in front, the minstrels last, between them maidens playing timbrels... There is Benjamin, the least of them, in the lead, the princes of Judah in their throng . . ."*

Then Jacob told them that he would soon die. He reminded them that they must take his remains back to the land of his fathers, back to the land of Canaan, in the cave in the field of Mach-pelah, where those he loved were buried. There they buried Abraham and Sarah, his wife; There they buried Isaac and Rebekah, his wife; and there he had buried Leah. When Jacob had finished giving all the instructions, and had finished all the blessings upon the heads of his sons, he relaxed upon his bed and there he died in the presence of the twelve tribes of Israel. Thus ended the age or dispensation of the patriarchs.

Joseph threw himself across the body of his father, and wept and kissed him. Later he commanded that the body be embalmed. This embalming process took approximately 40 days; they wept for 30 days, making a total of 70 days.

EGYPTIAN EMBALMING

The body was split open, and all internal organs were taken out. A hole was punched either in the roof of the mouth or in the back of the head, and the brains were drained out, (sometimes drawn through the nasal passages). The body was washed externally with water, then internally with palm-wine, oil of cedar and other antiseptic preparations. The body was then steeped in a strong infusion of niter. The time required for the niter treatment varied anywhere from 30 to 40 or even 70 days. Maybe it varied at different stages of Egyptian history. Also, the embalming process depended upon the family means.

When this was completed, the body and limbs were carefully wrapped in bandages of fine linen, plastered on the underside with gum, and it seemed to have been in some way subjected to extreme heat. Some have even conjectured that it was soaked in boiling hot pitch; hundreds of yards of cloth were wrapped around the body, plastered with lime on the inside. This cloth was painted and ornamented with different kinds of figures. The oldest mummy known to us is now in the British Museum. It is supposed to be one of the Pharaohs.

JACOB GOES HOME

Verse 4: And when the days of his mourning were past, Joseph spake unto the house of Pharaoh, saying, If now I have found grace in your eyes, speak, I pray you, in the ears of Pharaoh, saying,

Verse 5: My father made me swear, saying, Lo, I die: in my grave which I have digged for me in the land of Canaan, there shalt thou bury me. Now therefore let me go up I pray thee, and bury my father, and I will come again.

In chapter 50:4, we read, "*. . . spake unto the house of Pharaoh . . .*" Why couldn't Joseph speak directly to the Pharaoh, since he was second in command? He solicited the intervention of his friends in the court because his hair and beard had grown during the days of mourning; he was not in proper condition to approach the king according to the etiquette of the court.

Verse 6: And Pharaoh said, Go up, and bury thy father, according as he made thee swear.

When that caravan of mourners left Egypt, it was quite a sight to behold. He had all his house; all his brethren; his father's house; the servants of Pharaoh; the eldest of his house; and all the elders of the land of Egypt. Only the children and herds were left behind. A great company of people, chariots, and horsemen left Egypt to bury Jacob in Canaan.

At the threshing floor of Atad, which is beyond Jordan, they mourned for seven days. When the inhabitants of the land of Canaan saw this long procession, and heard all the mourning, they said one to another, *"This is a very grievous mourning brought upon the Egyptians."* Likely they had never witnessed such a funeral; it made such a lasting impression upon them, they renamed the place *"Anbel-mizraim"* which means *"Egyptian Mourners."* They said, *"It is a place of very deep mourning by these Egyptians."* The seven-day mourning period is still a part of Jewish tradition. They sit on the floor for seven days and seven nights and literally wail; often wailers are hired when the family is small.

And his sons did what he had commanded them to do. They carried him into the land of Canaan, and buried him in the cave of the field of Machpelah, which Abraham bought with the field for a possession of a burying place of Ephron the Hittite, in front of Mamre.

Then Joseph returned to Egypt. His brothers accompanied him back to Egypt; but they began to reason that since Jacob was dead, Joseph would try to seek revenge, because they had sold him into slavery. They lost no time reminding him that before Jacob died, he had left instructions that all should be forgiven.

Verse 17: So shall ye say unto Joseph, Forgive, I pray thee now, the trespass of thy brethren, and their sin; for they did unto thee evil: and now, we pray thee, forgive the trespass of the servants of the God of thy father. And Joseph wept when they spake unto him.

Verse 19: And Joseph said unto the, Fear not: for am I in the place of God?

His brothers not only asked for a full pardon, but they offered to be his slaves. He could not contain himself for he saw the sincerity of their petition, and loved them even more. He answered with a question which could be turned around to say, *"I am in the place where God put me. You thought you were doing evil against me, but God meant it for good, so I could keep you alive in the days of sore famine. Fear not for I will take care of you and all your little ones."* With this thought in mind, we can more fully understand Romans 8:28, *"And we know that all things work together for good to them that love God, to them who are the called according to his purpose."*

JOSEPH DIES

Joseph was 56 when Jacob died. He lived to be 110 (56 more years), then he died with a prophecy of their deliverance upon his lips.

Verse 24: And Joseph said unto his brethren, I die: and God will surely visit you, and bring you out of this land unto the land which he sware to Abraham, to Isaac, and to Jacob.

Verse 25: And Joseph took an oath of the children of Israel, saying, God will surely visit you, and ye shall carry up my bones from thence.

Verse 26: So Joseph died, being an hundred and ten years old: and they embalmed him, and he was put in a coffin in Egypt.

Joseph made his family promise that when God led them from Egypt, they would carry his body with them. They took an oath as he had done with Jacob; an oath that was finally fulfilled by their heirs 430 years later. There arose a Pharaoh in the land of Egypt that knew not Joseph, and he enslaved the children of Israel for centuries, until God sent Moses to lead them out; and in Exodus 13:19 we read, *"And Moses took the bones of Joseph with him: for he had straitly sworn the children of Israel, saying, God will surely visit you; and ye shall carry up my bones away hence with you."* The strict embalming process had preserved the bones of Joseph down in Egypt until the iniquity of the Amorites be fulfilled. *"But in the fourth generation they shall come hither again: for the iniquity of the Amorites is not yet full" (Genesis 15:16), and so be it.*

(1606 B.C.)

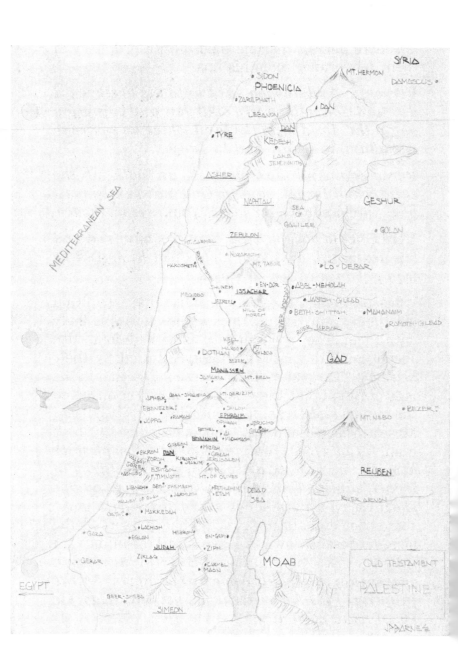

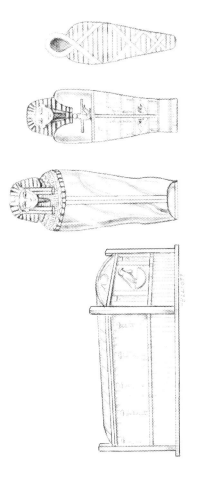

Embalming Process

"And Joseph went up to bury his father; and with him went up all the servants of Pharaoh, the elders of his house, and all the elders of the land of Egypt" (Genesis 50:7).